TWICE A HERO

T0385327

PHIL TOMKINS

Front cover: Hoisting the national flag on the Castle, Athlone, Co. Westmeath, Monday 28th February 1922.

L to R: Comdt. George Adamson, Commandant General Sean McEoin, Comdt. Tony Lawler, Divisional Adjutant; Company Comdt. Ned Cooney, Divisional Quartermaster; Comdt. Barney McGiffe and Captain Con Costello.

(Photograph Courtesy of The National Library of Ireland)

Back cover: Vickers Machine Gun and Crew, The Great War.

TWICE A HERO

One man's fight for freedom in the trenches of the
Great War and ditches of the Irish Midlands

PHIL TOMKINS

MEMOIRS

Cirencester

Published by Memoirs

MEMOIRS
PUBLISHING

25 Market Place, Cirencester, Gloucestershire, GL7 2NX
info@memoirsbooks.co.uk www.memoirspublishing.com

Copyright ©Phil Tomkins, October 2012

First published in England, October 2012

ISBN 9781909874084

Printed in England

The biography is dedicated to my maternal Grandmother Mrs Annie (Nan) Hewitt (nee Adamson), men and women of the Athlone Brigade Irish Republican Army and the many brave Irishmen of Kitchener's army who served in the Great War, who gave their lives in the mistaken belief that their sacrifice would lead to an independent Ireland.

ACKNOWLEDGMENTS

In the production of this biography, I have been materially assisted by many people in both a private and professional capacity. I would like to express gratitude to Gearoid O'Brien, Executive Librarian, Aidan Heavey Public Library, Athlone, Co. Westmeath who started me on my quest by providing the basis for this story. John Rattigan for his fount of local knowledge both pictorial, written and oral. Thanks to Simon Fowler, Ancestors Magazine, R.W. O'Hara, researcher, and the staff of the National Archives, Kew, London and the staff of the National Archives, Dublin. Staff of Tyldesley Library, Manchester, England. Jim Parker, Machine Gun Corps Research. Noelle Grothier, Archivist, Military Archives, Dublin, and Margaret Kilcommins, Pensions Administration Section Department of Defence, Renmore, Galway. My youngest son Philip for his IT skills and sound advice, cousins Lilly Slattery for her assistance and perseverance in obtaining pertinent military documents, Deirdre Twomey for her input of documents and family photographs, and Ann Brennan for her encouragement, and her 'home from home' during research in Ireland, Anne V James, copy editing and Anne Wittles, proof-reading. Family friend Max Vitali graphic designer for the splendid book cover. Not least my late grandmother Annie Hewitt (nee Adamson) to whom this work is dedicated.

Every effort has been made to ensure the accuracy of the events, people, and places in this book, and all original references have been acknowledged. Opinions expressed, or conclusions drawn, are solely my own.

FOREWORD

It is difficult to learn from history if we don't know what history is.

At the urging of my four children, all born and raised in England, I ventured into the genealogy of our Irish family. Eventually I came to the maternal line, the Adamsons of Moate, Co. Westmeath. I remembered little of the stories told to me by my grandmother Annie (Nan) Hewitt, nee Adamson, her sister Lucy and my great grandmother Elizabeth Adamson, about my granduncle George who had fought in The Great War and the Irish War of Independence. Other than that, and the obvious pride the family had in his achievements, I never got to know much more about him. I regretted not having listened attentively to accounts of their thoughts, and subsequent feelings. I wished that I had asked questions about him or really listened to the old folk as eventually they, and other crucial witnesses, all passed on, taking their memories with them. By now, 2008, the story of Uncle George seemed to be beyond reach, for he had faded into the wallpaper of life. My enquiries in the area eventually led me to his burial place in the disused and Godforsaken Dunegan Holy Trinity Cemetery, Mount Temple, Moate, Co. Westmeath, Eire. Unable to find any trace of his grave in the wilderness I was confronted with, I resolved to find out about this man, my own kith and kin, this obscure ancestor of mine and, if possible, write his story before it was lost forever to my children, family and history.

According to the great Russian writer Tolstoy, a drama does not tell us the whole of a person's life - what it does is place it in particular situations. Then, from the way the person deals with the situations, his character is revealed to us more fully. The following account is of a heroic young Irishman, a gallant soldier, patriot and rebel, why he fought, where, when, and how. The conditions he fought under and the men who lived and died beside him. It covers the seven hundred years struggle for a free and independent Ireland, two forgotten theatres of war in Salonika and Palestine, The Irish War of Independence and the Irish Civil War.

CHAPTER 1

The word 'story' is the second half of the word 'history'

(Unknown)

The .45-Calibre bullet, fired at close quarters, thumped into George Adamson's chest like a fist, driving the air out of him, forcing him to the ground. At the same time a round tore into the right arm of his companion Gerald Davis. For the two rebels, their spring day mission into the Athlone countryside had turned into a life-and-death situation. It was a good day gone wrong.

The year; 1921. The place; the Irish Midlands. The era; the height of the Irish struggle for Independence from Britain.

The shots were heard by another Active Service Unit (ASU) of the Irish Republican Army, under the command of Thomas 'Con' Costello. They had received information that British officers from the garrison in Athlone had a habit of going up the Shannon in a boat to fish on certain days. They were reported as always being armed.

The ASU decided to ambush them and mobilised on the banks of the river to 'do the job.' Their position compromised by the nearby gun battle less than half a mile away which could have alerted the officers, the ambush party made a hasty but disciplined withdrawal and rushed to the scene of the action.

George and Gerald were in the area to investigate a report that a spy was operating in Carricknoughton, but had the misfortune to tangle with two Tans (paramilitary police) paying court in a barnyard with two Athlone girls. It is highly probable that the young ladies in question were members of the Cumann na mBan (The League of Women) of the Irish Republican women's paramilitary organization, founded on 2nd April 1914. The Athlone Company came into being on the 11th April, 1915 to 'advance the cause of Irish liberty' as an auxiliary unit of the Irish Volunteers. They were employed with great success in obtaining information and intelligence from the Tans. The two rebels didn't get the best of the encounter. They held up the first Tan and disarmed him. Gerald left George, who was armed with a Parabellum automatic and the Tan's revolver, to stand guard on their captive while he went in search of his companion. Here is Gerald's account of the action that followed:

> '*This Tan was being a clomp of turf.*' (He had the girl he was with in front of him and was using her to cover him from being fired at. Davis was reluctant to fire as he might hit the girl.) '*I shouted "Hands Up" at him, but he fired at me* [hitting Gerald in the muscle of the right arm] *and then cleared off as I fired at him. I had a Colt revolver, but the ammunition I had was not the right type and this did not assist in accurate shooting. I hit him in the thigh with one of my shots but did not do him much harm. I heard Adamson shouting and, looking around, observed him on the ground with the Tan on top of him. The Tan was a powerful big Englishman and he had George down and had taken the gun off him and shot him through the chest* [and was in the act of putting another into him]. *I fired at this Tan and shot him through the back.*

The other Tan now came back and I fired at him, but missed him. I now helped Adamson to his feet and we both got away. Adamson had lost his gun, but I had retained mine and we had missed collecting the two guns belonging to the Tans also which we had hoped to do. Adamson was badly wounded in the chest and I was wounded in the fleshy portion of my arm.' (Gerald Davis, Witness Statement No: 13261 to the Bureau of Military History.)

The Tan's quick reaction to the rebel challenge to disarm them was, without doubt, that of highly trained and battle hardened soldiers of The Great War. The accuracy of their shooting leads to this conclusion. Luckily for George and Gerald, it would appear that the Tans judged them to be scouts for a much larger force and they quickly broke off the action and returned to their barracks in Athlone. It appears that no QRF (Quick Reaction Force) was sent out by the Tan command.

At the time of the incident, 23-year-old-George was a Vice Officer commanding the Athlone Brigade of the Irish Republican Army. His companion Gerald Davis was a county organiser from HQ Dublin. In January 1921, HQ asked for Volunteers to become county organisers and especially university students (Davis was a medical student at the National University Dublin). The candidates had to attend a series of lectures in guerrilla warfare, engineering, the construction of land mines and the use of arms. They were trained by Diamund Hegarty in explosives and Rory O'Connor in engineering. Gerald recorded his first meeting with George:

'When I eventually got in touch with the Volunteers I was very happy to leave Athlone. I left in a horse and cart with a farmer. I clubbed up with a chap called George Adamson.

3

*He was Vice Brigade O/C. and had served in the previous
or first world war. He was a fine type of man, well built,
a good athlete and a very good fellow all round. There was
no real active service unit or flying column in the brigade
area at this time. The brigade organisation was in a pretty
bad state. There had been a brigade column organised in
the area and they had carried out a few ambushes and lost
a few men killed. Following the intense activity after those
incidents, the column had got scattered and disorganised.
The Athlone area was a very difficult one to operate in.
The country is generally flat and boggy and there were no
mountains. Athlone was always a strong enemy garrison
centre and the people in the town were none too friendly
towards us, I suppose this applied to all garrison towns. The
people in the country, however, were generally all right and,
with occasional exceptions, could be relied upon. When I
got in touch with the Volunteers and especially Adamson,
I was feeling better* [about his task]. *The first thing I did
was to organise patrols around the town of Athlone in an
effort to ambush Tans. The enemy were not contacted,
however, except on one occasion by Adamson and me.'*

*(Gerald Davis, Witness Statement No: 1361 to the
Bureau of Military History.)*

In the case of the badly wounded George, he was spirited away from
the scene across the Shannon by the ASU ambush party and placed
with the O'Connor's in their home, in Derrevane, Tombeagh about
three miles from Ballycumber in County Offaly, where he received
medical attention. This isolated cottage was situated in the centre
of Lemanaghan bog and used by men 'on the run.' The O'Connor's
were relatives of Tom 'Con' Costello (Commanding Officer of the

Athlone Brigade, Irish Republican Army). Gerald's arm went septic for a while, but eventually got better.

As George was nursed back to health from his serious and near deathly wound, the bullet, because of its large diameter, created a deep and substantial permanent wound channel, which lowered his blood pressure rapidly having entered and exited through a lung. He had ample time to reflect over the intervening years and wonder at the irony of his many miraculous escapes from wounding and death during his service as a British soldier in The Great War, only to suffer a gunshot wound in his own home county.

CHAPTER 2

There is nothing stronger than the heart of a Volunteer.

In 1912, when British Prime Minister Asquith introduced his Home Rule Bill for Ireland, the country was part of the United Kingdom governed from the Houses of Parliament in Westminster, London. Ireland was represented in the British parliament by 105 MPs. About a third of them were Unionists from Northern Ireland, but the majority were members of the Irish Parliamentary Party, commonly known as the Home Rule Party, based in Southern Ireland. Its declared primary aim was *'to secure and maintain the rights and liberties common to the whole people of Ireland'*.

The Bill, also known as the (Irish) Third Home Rule Bill, and formally known as The Government of Ireland Act 1914, was intended to provide self-government for Ireland within the United Kingdom of Great Britain and Ireland. On the 25th May 1914 it was passed for its final stage.

In the two years before the outbreak of the Great War, Home Rule looked bound to come to Ireland. Unionists were quick to respond, forming the Ulster Volunteer Force, running guns to equip it and defend the Union with Britain. This group eventually attained a membership in the region of 90,000.

The Irish Volunteers (Oglaigh na hEireann) were formed by Eoin Mac Neill in November 1913, in the face of opposition from the Ulster Volunteer Force. He was helped by Sir Roger Casement who co-wrote the Volunteer's manifesto. They were fully committed to securing and supporting the democratic advent of Home Rule. In July 1914 Casement travelled to the U.S. to promote and raise money for the Volunteers. Through his friendship with such men as Bulmer Hobson, who was a member of the Volunteers and the Irish Republican Brotherhood (IRB), Casement established connections with exiled Irish nationalists, in particular Clan na Gael.

At this point Ireland was close to civil war, but the beginning of the Great War dramatically intervened. In September 1914 the Ulster Volunteer Force demonstrated its commitment to The Crown as the whole membership joined the British Army to support the war effort.

The action taken by the Ulster Volunteers was followed by a call to arms by John Redmond MP, who was the elected leader of the Irish Parliamentary Party. He endorsed enlistment after Home Rule was given the Royal Assent on the 18th September 1914, when it was placed on the statute book that its legal effect, as well as an Ulster provision, would follow the war's conclusion. He called on all the members of the Irish Volunteers to join the British Army, seeing this course of action as the best choice in ensuring the enactment of Home Rule at war's end. He was most influential and highly successful in urging Irishmen to support the war effort. In his first speech on the subject, on 20th September 1914, which he made in the village of Woodbridge in County Wicklow, he called on the Volunteers to *'account yourselves as men not only in Ireland but wherever the firing line extends in defence of right, of freedom and religion in this war'*.

He is quoted as saying:

> *'The interests of Ireland – of the whole of Ireland – are at stake in this war. This war is undertaken in defence of the highest interests of religion and morality and right, and it would be a disgrace for ever to our country, a reproach to her manhood, and a denial of the lessons of her history if young Ireland confined their efforts to remaining at home to defend the shores of Ireland from an unlikely invasion, and shirking from the duty of proving on the field of battle that gallantry and courage which have distinguished their race all through its history.'*

Some 69,000 Catholic and 53,000 Protestant men, from both North and South, volunteered to fight in the Great War for the freedom of small nations. Encouraged by John Redmond, this figure included some 24,000 Irish Volunteers, to which George belonged.

The Volunteers split after John Redmond's repeated calls for support of the British war effort. The majority took sides with the Redmond cause and became what was known as the National Volunteers. The minority, some 12,000 men, remained loyal to the Irish Volunteers. They set up a Military Council in 1915 headed by Patrick Pearse with the purpose of gaining full independence for Ireland, by force if necessary. Typical of the time, the Drumraney Company, Co. Westmeath, Volunteers held a referendum to decide which side they would support. Sixteen of the thirty-three Volunteers voted for Redmond and enlisted in the British Army. Seventeen voted against the motion and as a result, got to keep the eight rifles in the company's possession. George, an idealist and already an Irish Volunteer, took part in the voting by all units throughout Ireland in response to Redmond's appeal. This, when Ireland was the only home nation where conscription was not in force.

In general, the majority of the new recruits had the support of the Irish people. They believed that they were fighting for a free Ireland in a free Europe. While some men joined out of economic necessity and others, in the hope that the experience of serving side by side against a common enemy, would create friendships that could transcend historic differences.

Thomas Kettle, the former nationalist MP for East Tyrone who served and was killed as a Lieutenant in the 9th Royal Dublin Fusiliers, stated:

> *'Used with wisdom which is sown in tears and blood, this tragedy of Europe may be and must be the prologue to the two reconciliations of which all statesmen have dreamed, the reconciliation of Protestant Ulster with Ireland and the reconciliation of Ireland with Great Britain.'*

The Irish recruits to the British Army were young men in their late teens, a mix of rural labourers, urban unskilled workers and long-term unemployed, the majority of whom were fit and healthy, more so than their English counterparts. Most of the farm boys were experienced in the use of weapons, mainly shotguns, and many of the urban boys belonged to one of the growing gun clubs in Ireland, not to mention one of the many private armies operating at the time. Irish Volunteer, eighteen years-old George Adamson, was just one of the thousands of young Irishmen throughout Ireland who answered John Redmond's call to arms. On the 19th February 1915 he enlisted as a volunteer in the British Army.

CHAPTER 3

THE ADAMSONS

Crux Mini Grata Quies

(The Cross gives me welcome rest)

In each family a story is playing itself out, and each family's story embodies its hope and despair.

(Aguste Napier)

The Adamsons can trace their history in Ireland back to the time of the Plantation in 1678. The Plantations started in 1609 when some 500,000 acres in Ulster was made available for settlement by English Protestants and Scottish Presbyterian's in Ulster, Northern Ireland, to displace Irish Catholics and strengthen English Rule. Further such plantations were authorized in the Midlands and in about 1678 George Adamson's ancestors arrived from Scotland and settled in Clonegan and Nahod in Co. Westmeath. The county is situated in east-central Ireland. It covers an area of 710 sq. miles. Its principal towns are Athlone, which straddles the River Shannon, Castle Pollard, Kilbeggan, Moate, Mullingar and Tyrells Pass.

Through an act of parliament, they dispossessed the local farmers in order to settle in the town and surrounding areas and carry on farming, increasing acreage by reclaiming bog-land. In time they became 'as Irish as the Irish themselves'. However, many of the native Irish suffered hunger and deprivation because of dispossession during this period and could not, or would not ever, accept Britain's right to steal their land and homes.

George was born in the small 12th century Norman market town of Moate, County Westmeath in the Irish Midlands in 1897 to Joseph (Joe) and Elizabeth Adamson (nee Downey) whose parents were John and Mary Downey (nee Horan). He was christened into the Catholic Church, his Grandfather Thomas having converted to Catholicism. Joe was a shoemaker (cobbler), a hard-working God-fearing family man.

Elizabeth, a fine, strong, resolute country-woman of great dignity who, up to her 80s, tended her vegetable garden dressed in button-up ankle shoes with her skirts tied up as she turned the soil, planted and harvested her crop. She could use a spade and a hoe as good as any man. Her innate strength she passed on to her sons. Still hale and hearty into old age, she died one week to the day after the tragic death of her beloved grandson Tommy McGuinness in the Curragh Camp, Co. Kildare and is buried in Newbridge Cemetery Co. Kildare.

His parents christened their second son George Joseph Adamson. The family originally lived in 118 Moategranoge, Moate, later moving to a small house on the North side of the Athlone Road in Moate, halfway between the Gap House and the Hall Road. Aged about seven years, he attended the boys' school in what is now St. Patrick's Hall. Here, his pals Jim Tormey and Kit McKeown, both to play important parts in his life. On leaving school and finding jobs to be scarce, he worked as a labourer in the local area for a few years prior to his enlistment in the British Army. He spoke Gaelic and was involved with the local branch of the Gaelic Athletic Association and the Irish games of Gaelic football and hurling. An excellent all-round athlete, he was at a high standard of fitness at the time.

CHAPTER 4

There is nothing so likely to produce peace as to be well prepared to meet the enemy

(George Washington)

George volunteered for the British Army on Friday 19th February 1915 at Athlone, County Westmeath. He declared his age as 18 years and ten months. On the 20th February 1915 George, as Private 4941, was posted to the 5th (Extra Reserve) Battalion, the Prince of Wale's Leinster Regiment (Royal Canadians), a depot/training unit stationed at Passage West Co. Cork, Southern Ireland. He was given weapon training on the .303 calibre Lee Enfield rifle, along with general infantry training, foot and weapon drill, battle tactics and trench digging in the local area near Monkstown Castle. His pay as a Private soldier: thirty shillings a week. During recruit training, he was found to be an excellent shot with the rifle to marksmanship level, a qualification which earned him proficiency pay and a place in the battalion machine-gun section.

A machine-gun is a rapid firing, crew-served small arm that can provide continuous bursts of automatic fire. It was used in the Great War as an integral part of infantry tactics. In the first year of the war, all infantry battalions were equipped with a machine-gun section of two guns, which increased to four guns in February 1915.

Eventually promoted to Gunner, George had the job of carrying the tripod which weighed 22 kg. With his vital statistics on enlistment 5 feet 7 inches in height, with a chest measurement of 35 inches, one wonders how he managed to carry any of the components of the weapon, let alone the tripod. It was deemed impossible to hold the weapon against the rebound or recoil, unless the firer was really fit. George's build belied a strength beyond his years; he was indeed one hard man, as he was to prove time and again.

In May 1915 he moved, with his battalion, from Passage West to Plymouth in the South of England for further training. When the 5th Battalion moved to Mullingar in Southern Ireland in September 1915, George was posted to the 6th Service (meaning wartime service only) Battalion, The Leinster Regiment, 29th Brigade, 10th (Irish) Division, the Mediterranean East Expeditionary Force on the 24th September. He and his fellow replacements were sent out to join their battalions by the long sea route via Gibraltar and Malta, a journey which could take up to ten days on a zigzag voyage to avoid German submarines through the Aegean to their destination, the Isle of Lemnos, arriving on the 2nd October 1915.

The 10th (Irish) Division was formed on 29th August, 1914 as part of the First New Army. It was primarily recruited from the ranks of Redmond's National Volunteers but initially included a large number of battalions from Great Britain, bringing Irishmen of different social classes, political opinions and religions together. It moved to the Curragh Camp, Newbridge and Kildare in Southern Ireland, where training in Brigade strength began; the Division was part of Kitchener's Army.

It consisted of a large number of battalions from Britain, with a combined force of many Irish Regiments; 5th Connaught Rangers, (nicknamed 'The Devil's Own'); Royal Dublin Fusiliers (named 'The Blue caps' from the regiment's time in India when the wearing of a blue cap was a symbol of an elite force); Inniskilling Fusiliers, (or 'The Skins' as they were known); Lenister Regiment; Royal Munster Fusiliers (better known as 'The Dirty Shirts' from their time in India, in storming a fort their shirts were covered in blood, dirt and sweat); 5th Royal Irish Regiment and 6th Royal Irish Rifles (or just The Rifles). In May 1915 the Division moved to Basingstoke in Southern England. There on the 28th and 29th May they were seen by the King and on 1st June, they were inspected by Lord Kitchener at Hackwood Park.

On 27th June 1915 the Division received orders to prepare for service overseas. This was confirmed on the 1st July 1915 as detailed for service in the Gallipoli peninsula in the south of Turkey. Lightweight khaki drill clothing was issued and embarkation began on 9th July 1915 at Liverpool Docks, setting sail for the port of Mudros south of the Aegean island of Lemnos in Greece, which lies close to the entrance of the straits of the Dardanelles. The Division was the first all-Irish formation to take to the field of war.

On 6th and 7th August the Division, less 29th Brigade, landed on Gallipoli in the Dardanelles at Sulva Bay with the Brigade later seeing action on Sari Bair and Hill 60 and Chunuk Bair peak. In September 1915 when the Sulva front became a stalemate, the tattered and battered remnants of the 10th Division, having taken heavy casualties in the bitter fighting with the Turks, left Gallipoli on the 29th and sailed to back to Mudros. The island was used as a harbour and for preparing operations in the Dardanelles. Here they had only four days to rest, making up deficiencies and regrouping, as 90% of the Division had been slaughtered, wounded or had fallen ill whilst fighting the Turks. All of its constituent battalions had to be reinforced and hastily re-organised before being dispatched to join the Angelo-French Expeditionary Force that had been assembled in Greece to fight the Bulgarian Army in Serbia.

At Mudros, the new draft which included machine gunner Private George Adamson, was incorporated into the 6th Battalion The Lenister Regiment. The re-enforcements affixed green coloured shoulder tags to their epaulettes denoting that they now belonged to 10th (Irish) Division.[1]

[1] When up to strength the British army structure during The Great War was as follows; Company 227 all ranks – Battalion 1007 – Brigade 4005 – Division 18,179.

CHAPTER 5

A long way from home in a battle zone

As fierce fighting was going on in Gallipoli, in another war Austrian forces had invaded Serbia and were now pushing on to Macedonia on the Serbian-Greek border. Watching both the Gallipoli action and the Austrian invasion in Serbia was King Ferdinand of (neutral) Bulgaria, who laid claim to part of Macedonia. Seeing an opportunity to settle old scores, Ferdinand sided with Germany and Austria-Hungary. He mobilised his army and reserves and joined the German war effort in October 1915 by invading Serbia from the east. It was impossible for Serbia to hold their northern frontier against the Austria-Germans and handle the new threat from the Bulgars. This led Serbia to appeal to the British and French governments for military assistance. At the same time, Greece asked the Allies for help with their treaty obligations to Serbia.

Each did send help, but it was inadequate to save Serbia from its fate. At the eleventh hour, after Bulgaria had mobilised, the Allies resolved to land a small combined British and French force at Salonika which ports, although neutral, offered the most convenient base for operations in support of Serbia. The initial help consisted of one French Division from Cape Hellas and the 10th (Irish) Division, hurriedly dispatched in an effort to stop the Serbian retreat. Following regrouping, on the evening of 4th

October 1915 George's battalion embarked on the H.M.S. *Albion* for Salonika (now Thessalonika), capital of Macedonia and the nation's largest region, where they remained for almost two years.

After the eighty-mile sea voyage from Mudros, with no lights showing on the ship and smoking by the troops banned due to the fear of submarines, the troopship sailed through the slowly narrowing Gulf of Therma. It threaded its way perilously under escort through anti-submarine nets at nightfall. It finally anchored beyond Karaburun where the lights of Salonika could be seen five miles beyond the bay. Next morning with the sun high in the sky, George could see the gleaming city spread out across the water with its long strand and famous White Tower, its quay and clustering minarets. To a country boy from a small provincial market town in Ireland, it must have had a startling effect.

George would have been struck by the feverish activity of the picket boats and miniature launches that rushed, hither and thither on various errands among the vessels anchored around the bay. Next came the raising of the anchor and the approach to the quay and the landing, toward late afternoon on the 5th October 1915, with the Leinsters first to disembark. This was followed by a march through streets which he would have found to be narrow and filthy, thronged with the most diversely garbed individuals, and smelling of all the vilest odours of the East – a mixture of rotting refuse, perfumes and spices. As he was marched outside the city to a camp on the Seres road, he would have seen the desolate, parched moorland looping from gully to gully.

Also the flat plain of the Vardar, gradually alternating from the flat alluvial plain to a country of woods and hills, to the distant background of snow-clad Mount Olympus, surrounded by rugged mountains from which the barbarians and brigands in former days constantly harassed the city.

The native populations were mainly Greeks and Turks, with the proportion of both nationalities being equal. There was little trouble between them and it was quite usual to find a village divided by its main street into two distinct parts, of which one would be Greek and the other Turkish. Law and order such as there was, was the single unifying principle. George was to find the Turks to be friendly, while the Greeks were cold and hostile.

Tragedy struck when D Battery (6 Guns) of the Royal Artillery, newly assigned to the 10th Division, embarked for Salonika in the *Marquette*, and on the 23rd October when off Salonika the *Marquette* was torpedoed. The Battery lost 100 men, all the animals, (horses and mules) the guns and equipment. However, by 24th October the bulk of the 10th Division (400 Officers and 13,000 men) had landed at Salonika.

The British and French forces were there at the invitation of the Greek Prime Minister Eleutherios Venizelos, whose party was pro-British and anxious to enter the war with the Allies. However, the Greeks were divided in their loyalties.

The king and his party, nominally friends of the Allies, were in fact very pro-German, King Constantine being married to the Kaiser's daughter. Therefore, they were very upset by the landings, to the extent that the Chief of the General Staff, General Dousmanis in Athens, told the commanders of the British-Franco force: *'You will be driven into the sea, and you will not have time to even cry for mercy.'*

CHAPTER 6

SALONIKA & MACEDOINA 1916 – 1917

What doesn't kill us – makes us stronger

(Friedrich Nietzche)

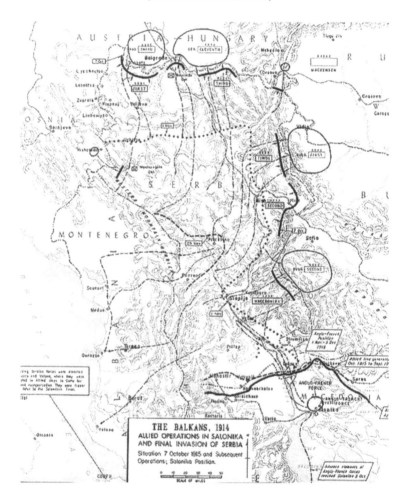

THE BALKANS, 1914
ALLIED OPERATIONS IN SALONIKA
AND FINAL INVASION OF SERBIA
Situation 7 October 1915 and Subsequent
Operations; Salonika Position.

From the onset, the Allies were compelled to carry out operations at a great disadvantage. All that seemed possible was the use of the only existing railway northwards and push their comparatively small force rapidly up to the Vardar valley to assist the hard pressed, retreating Serbs. Accordingly, the French Division was sent by rail and speedily occupied positions to create a formidable diversion against the Bulgarian flank as possible. After about ten days, on the 13th November, the 10th Division followed by entraining at Salonika and de-training at Doiran that night, the journey having taken eleven hours on the single-track railway. From there, they marched towards the Greco-Serbian frontier through the valleys on muddied, potholed tracks. After weeks of severe cold the ground was frozen solid, which made progress tough going for the infantrymen and their pack-mules. The area, with its barren hill-tops and deep gullies, was almost devoid of any vegetation. In atrocious weather conditions, they climbed into the snow-covered mountain region of Southern Serbia.

On the 19th November, the 10th Division began relieving the French at Kosturino, due north of Lake Doiran where the 6th Leinsters took over the line from Causli to the lake. The Division was to operate easterly of the Doiran-Strumnitza road. Their aim was to relieve the French and the protecting force it had thrown out on its right flank covering the area of Kosturino – Doiran and if possible to take the high ground from the enemy.

The Division took up positions and established a trench line on the new front during the nights of 20th and 21st November, coming face to face with the Bulgarians for the first time. There, they became responsible for part of a ten-mile line between Kosturino in the north and in a south-easterly direction towards Lake Doiran, parallel to the Bulgaria frontier.

Their entrenched positions were on the Dedeli Ridge on the far side of Bojimia Valley and the Kosturino Ridge. The positions lay in the heart of a steep, confused, rocky mass of mountains. Divisional H.Q. at Dedeli overlooked the half-mile broad valley and the Bojimia River, whose bed was a dry waste of sand and rock. On the ridge at the far side of the valley lay their entrenched positions. The ground was of unrelenting rock, so hard to work that the French had relied chiefly on sangers or stone redoubts. These were not deep and liable to splinter under shell fire. The Irish didn't occupy them, but left them empty to draw the enemy's artillery fire. The Bulgarians, estimated at 10,000 strong, of the 2nd Philipopolis Division, were holding a line of blockhouses and trenches along a ridge parallel to and facing the Irish. They were spread out between the Greek frontier and Strumniza. However, comparatively calm conditions prevailed until the end of November.

While exposed on the ridge, George and his fellow soldiers were hit by a blizzard which lasted for three days. It began on the 27th November with sheeting rain, which turned into blinding snow. The temperature dropped as low -7.5F / 13.6C. George's only protection from the bitter cold and piercing wind was his groundsheet draped over his open trench and held down by heavy rocks. At times the weight of the snow caused the groundsheet to collapse into the trench giving him and his gun crew a thorough soaking. They then had the unenviable task of replacing the groundsheet in the teeth of the blizzard and shovelling out the snow from their trench. His comrades had to stand in the freezing snow and slush unable to change their wet and frozen lightweight clothing, as there was nothing to change into.

There were hundreds of cases of frostbite in the Division, with men frozen stiff and having to be stretchered back to first-aid posts to be revived. George wasn't one of them as he was young, supremely fit and fresh out of England and clothed in the warm battle dress as worn in the UK. The Division was depleted and physically weakened by its sheer exacting service at Sulva Bay when this devastating ordeal was thrust on them. They looked worse than they had at Sulva. The faces of most of them were yellow and wizened and their bodies thin. The trying climate of The Gallipoli Peninsula had sapped their strength and they were finding it difficult to cope.

Warm underclothing did eventually reach the Division, warm winter caps with ear-flaps, leather jerkins and field boots, but the middle of a snowstorm and the bitter cold prevented troops from undressing to put them on. Unfortunately there was no choice but to hold out in the freezing, shelter-less mountains as long as the French required protection, after which they could fall back within the Greek frontier.

During this period George had his first, but by no means last, confrontation with authority and King's Rules and Regulations (Army). It was to prove to be a brutal experience. The British Army discipline is very strict and a soldier has to be darned careful to stay on the narrow path of military virtue as there are numerous ways of breaking the rules. On the 3rd December 1915 he was 'Crimed' (put on a charge) with the offence of *'disregarding Trench Standing Orders'* as discipline in trench warfare was seen to be of vital importance. The Company Sergeant-Major kept what is known as Crime Sheets.

When a man committed a crime he was 'Crimed', that is, his name, number, and offence was entered on a Crime Sheet. The next day at 9 a.m. the accused would go before his Captain, who would set his punishment. At a subsequent brief hearing George was given 28 days Field Punishment No.1, which was sanctioned by the Commanding Officer (battalion). However, with the imminent attacks by the Bulgarians his punishment was postponed

until a more suitable time and place. The next day he had more to
worry about than Field Punishment No.1.

On 4th December 1915 the Bulgarians, supported by their
mountain artillery, began to attack the Kosturino Ridge, adding to
the misery of the steadfast Irish troops. Luckily, due to fog that had
started on the 2nd December, their fire was for the most part
inaccurate. On 4th December, the Bulgar artillery fire began to be
better directed and concentrated, and it became apparent that they
had received reinforcements.

When it was realised that the Bulgars were about to make an
attack in force, General Mahon, Commander of the 10th Division,
asked General Sarrail the French Commander to speed up as much
as possible the retreat which was now in progress under the most
difficult conditions. The continuing withdrawal of the Serbs,
followed by the French through the Irish lines towards the
Macedonian border, was an extremely difficult and perilous
operation at that time of the year. It was exceedingly skilfully
carried out despite constant pressure from the Bulgarians. The Irish,
entrenched in thick mist and fog on the Serbian side of the Greek
border, continued to hold the line to allow the French and Serbian
troops to pass through in safety. Finally, on the afternoon of the
6th December, an exceptionally large force of Bulgarian troops
attacked the 10th Division positions. Backed by day-and-night
artillery bombardments and machine-gun fire and aided by fog,
they assaulted the frozen trenches of George's Division.

George, with a canvas belt of 250 rounds already loaded into his
gun, would have pulled back the crank handle twice to load the
breech. Sitting stiffly upright with the gun between his knees, his
lower-body thrust against the frozen earth, he would be gripping the
machine-gun handles to cut down on the vibration. With both
hands on the traversing handles, he would sight on a group of enemy

soldiers as they climbed through the drifting fog and smoke like wraiths. He would hook his fingers through the safety guard and press his thumbs down on the firing button. The gun would stutter, then start to clatter and hammer as George traversed back and forth, the flame from the gun barrel lighting up the wintry darkness.

The gun's barrel spewing out six hundred rounds per minute would set the Bulgars jerking and tumbling under fire like dancing men, or puppets in a Punch and Judy show. Meanwhile, George's Number 3 would be dragging up a second box of ammo as his Number 2 fed another belt of ammo into the weapon and George would have waited for the reload in frustration, and maybe a little fear. Finally, he would feel the tap on his shoulder and hear the words '*loaded and cocked*' from Number 2. Once again, a solid stream of bullets would pour from the weapon like a jet of water from a fire hose.

That night the enemy crept along the ravines that surrounded the peak and took it by storm at 5.30 on the morning of 7th December. About thirty Irish soldiers were captured but the rest got away. The loss gave the Bulgars a serious footing in the Irish line. They brought up their mountain artillery and machine-guns to the peak and began to enfilade (gunfire directed along the length of an enemy battle line) down the front of 30th Brigade.

During 7th to 8th December the Division fought in the Battle of Kosturino Ridge, where two attacks were made on the Irish trenches by a largely superior force of Bulgarians and their German allies, but these were driven off. This was followed by an all-night artillery bombardment strangely muffled by the fog and it continued with enough severity to stop supplies from reaching the Irish lines. During 8th December, heavy artillery and machine-gun fire rained in on the defensive positions. During the night the Irish had been reinforced by three French companies and a mountain battery (artillery).

The fog grew constantly denser and in the broken country of steep, twisting ravines and pathless hill-sides it was difficult to know where the enemy were going to attack next and surround the Irish and French. In the fierce battles that followed the vastly outnumbered Irish sustained heavy losses but they held the line. The worst attacks were the bayonet charges, where wounded men bled to death in the snow. In the initial attacks the Bulgarians gave no quarter, took no prisoners and killed the wounded.

Finally the order came for withdrawal, during which George's 29th Brigade were acting under the orders of General Leblois commanding the 57th French Division. On the morning of the withdrawal, the Bulgarians captured a trench in an advanced post known as the Rocky Peak, which was situated eight hundred yards north of Memsili. The effect of this being occupied by the Irish had denied the enemy artillery access to the right flank of 30th Brigade. The hill had originally been covered with a company of the Irish Fusiliers, but there was no cover there; it was nothing but a treeless, shelter-less, boulder-strewn height. The battalion had suffered so severely during the blizzard that this isolated position was withdrawn and only one company and one machine-gun was left to hold it. In their first attack the Bulgars captured one small trench, but were later driven out and off the hill at bayonet point.

The Bulgar attack on Rocky Peak might well have brought about disaster. Fierce fighting continued that evening and all the next day, when the troops of the 10th Division fell back to a line through Dedeli and Causli, just north of the Doiran-Strumnitza road. On 9th December the Causli was reorganised, the 6th Royal Irish Rifles being moved up in support of the 6th Leinster Regiment. On the night of 11th December, the 10th Division was given the order to retire across the Greco-Serbian frontier. At the cost of heavy losses from fatal wounds, frostbite and other sickness and realising the danger they were in, they withdrew. Before retiring, the Irish emptied their rifles into the enemy and used fixed bayonets, eventually making good their retreat over the border.

They were attacked as they crossed and some soldiers were taken captive. Irish casualties for this action were put at 1,300, with 300 men dead and the remainder wounded or taken prisoner. George's machine-gun had been gainfully employed throughout the actions of his unit. For this battle, infantry regiments within the 10th Division were awarded the battle honour *Kosturino*.

The move was at a critical time, as the roads were choked with British and French guns and troops moving into position. They had to march across the country by compass, but the march discipline was excellent and before dawn the 29th Brigade were in their new positions. At this stage it was not known if the enemy would enter Greek territory. A War Office report stated:

> *'After violent attacks by the enemy in overwhelming numbers, the 10th (Irish) Division, with the help of reinforcements, succeeded in retiring to a strong position from Lake Doiran westwards towards the Vardar valley.'*

Luckily, the Bulgarians having advanced down the Strumnitza road stopped just short of the Greek frontier stone, on the outskirts of Doiran town. They did not advance on Salonika but instead consolidated their gains in Macedonia. The Austrians, Bulgars, Germans and Turks were now able to establish themselves in formidable defensive positions to guard what they had won.

This, the Division's first encounter with the Bulgarians, had not been one of unmitigated satisfaction but at the same time there were many sound reasons for considering that it had made the best of very unfavourable conditions. The worn-out Division came down from the mountains by road in a terrible night march made in heavy rain, on roads already cut to pieces by heavy military traffic. Finally, the 6th Leinsters entrained at Sarigeul for Salonika and went into camp at Kapudjilar just outside the city. It then moved up to hold a line along the lakes across to the village of Skala Stavros, which was to be made part of the entrenched camp to be known as *The Birdcage*.

CHAPTER 7

FIELD PUNISHMENT

Let the punishment be proportionate to the offence.
(Marcus Tulius Cicero)

When flogging in the British Army came to an end in 1881, a new way of dealing with soldiers found guilty of minor offences on field service was introduced. This punishment was called Field Punishment Number One and involved the offender being attached to a fixed object for two hours a day, for any period up to three months. During the Great War, men who were given this sentence were sometimes placed within sight and range of enemy snipers and shell-fire. This punishment could be given for relative trivial offences such as incorrect dress, untidy appearance, loss of personally-issued clothing and equipment, not saluting or addressing superiors correctly, dirty or incorrect equipment or being late on parade. For instance, while in a front-line trench, orders forbade a soldier from taking off his boots, puttees, uniform, or equipment.

The system that tried and convicted George was, as in all armies, governed by regulations and military law. The British Army Manual of Military Law, which stipulated the punishment that was awarded to a soldier who broke any of its many rules and regulations, has always been an extension of criminal law.

This means that there are military offences in addition to those that would be tried by a civil court. It is not the same as the civil courts, with the crucial difference between the two being that under civil law the accused is held to be innocent until proven guilty, whereas in military law, George was regarded as being guilty until proven innocent.

Another salient point was that the unit commander conducting the hearing is the judge. There is no jury and extremely little chance of appeal, although the right of appeal is included in the regulations. The British Army was at the time composed of volunteers and as such, they were regarded as lower beings not fit for the niceties of British justice.

This attitude by the officer corps had a major effect on the outcome of the hearing, to George's detriment. For minor offences to do with King's Regulations, Standing Orders and Unit Routine Orders, the Company Commander could give the following sentence: *'Field punishment up to 28 days to a soldier not being a NCO (on field service).'* (George, was a Private soldier on active field service.)

The punishment would have taken place some time after the battle for Kosturino on 7th and 8th December 1915 and the subsequent retreat back into Greece at Kapudilar. As there was no Glass House (prison or detention centre) or permanent camp, sentences had to be carried out in the field, hence the name field punishment.

Field Punishment Number One, often abbreviated to 'F.P.No.1' or even just 'No.1', consisted of George, now back on Greek territory with his Division, being placed in fetters, handcuffs, or similar restraints. He was then attached by the ankles and wrists, standing up and spread-eagled to a fixed object, usually a gun-limber wheel. The punishment lasted for up to two hours a day, one hour in the morning and one hour in the afternoon. The restraints restricted circulation to the hands and feet and the pain after release, as the blood flow returned, was excruciating. The punishment of being manacled thus was applied to George for up to three days out of four, 28 days in total. As well as this he was drilled at high speed in full pack and rifle, and fed on water, bully beef and biscuits. Any spare time would be spent on hard labour, trench digging and repair and making of sandbag emplacements for the machine guns. On top of this George would have had to engage in all raids, working parties in No Man's Land and every hazardous undertaking that came along. All this, while exposed to the elements of a harsh winter.

The idea of this was to make a spectacle of George and to humiliate him in front of his mates. This was intensely disliked and resented by his fellow soldiers, who nicknamed it 'Crucifixion'. It has been alleged that this cruel and archaic process was sometimes applied within the view of the enemy and within the range of their guns. Although the 1914 manual of Military Law specifically stated that Field Punishment should not be applied in such a way as to cause physical harm, the procedure was never officially standardised and in practice, abuses were commonplace. While this punishment may appear to be very severe, it is actually quite lenient as most offences at the front carried a penalty of fourteen years imprisonment. Many units imposed tough discipline at the start of their operations as a way of setting an example.

It is said that Field Punishment No.1 was not very terrible physically, but most galling and humiliating mentally. It was believed that such a punishment exposed the real core of the soldier, and if that core were strong to start with, it became stronger. However, lashing men to a wheel was one of the most disgraceful things in war, yet it still continued until 1917 when the War Minister put a stop to it following protests in Parliament. One wonders at George's state of mind and health after such an ordeal. This one terrible incident in his life reveals a great deal about him, about his strength of character and his toughness. It appears that George had a stubborn streak in him that could flare up when he felt he was being unfairly treated.

The British army at that time expected dumb obedience from its common soldiery. Therefore this must have been very difficult for George to contend with, as it appears that at several times during his service, a clash of wills with authority occurred. There is no doubt that he was a good soldier, as despite further run-ins with authority he was promoted and demoted only to be promoted again on a number of occasions.

CHAPTER 8

BIRDCAGE

The harder the conflict, the more glorious the triumph.

(Thomas Paine)

As the Bulgarians did not follow up on their initial success, and it having been decided to hold Salonika, there was a rush to complete its defences so the Allies could advance into northern and western Greece. This they did during the first four months of 1916, where they were deployed to establish an advance system of defensives, to include lines of barbed wire entanglements, concealed trenches and concrete gun emplacements. The line, in a bastion about eight miles north of Salonika stretched for some 60 miles across the country. It was created by connecting with the Vardar marshes, a fifteen-mile depth of impassable morass in the west and using as a natural barrier the two great lakes of Langaza and Besliek in the east to the Gulf of Orfani at the steep, rocky valley known as the Rendina Gorge which was seven miles in length. On Christmas Day 1915, George and the Brigade were ordered to occupy the extreme right of the new defensive line. The distance to the shores of Lake Orfani was fifty miles over poor roads.

The move was to be made by sea. On 29th December the Brigade, after ten days rest from its labours in a camp outside Salonika, marched down to English Quay and embarked on the *Prince Abbas* which rounded the bay south of Chalcidicean Peninsula to the mouth of the Struma River. Disembarking on the next afternoon at Skala Stavros, they bivouacked on the beach. Then, on the last day of the year they marched up the Rendina Gorge.

On either side of the gorge through which the river flows were foothills and wooded ravines, bounded on the north and south by high mountains and plateaux. There they prepared to man outposts on the hills to the north of it. It was back to digging-in again and living in redoubts, (little iron tunnels, cubby holes, and small dugouts or shelters) in the side wall of a trench. H.Q. was camped near the river bank, pitched on a slope of land from where water seemed to ooze perpetually. There appeared to be springs and rivulets everywhere. In a consequence it was pretty well waterlogged; even the floor of the H.Q. was not without puddles.

There the Brigade was held with comparatively little activity. Adding to the misery the blizzards returned again followed by cold, driving rain which flooded the trenches. The 'bivvy' sheets proved to be useless against the incessant downpour. An icy wind, called the Vardar wind by the troops, came off the mountains from the north along with very severe weather, with heavy snowstorms freezing everything including George's army goatskin or sheepskin jerkin. He would have been acutely conscious of the snakes of rain that wriggled down his collar. The meat pudding, which was part of the British army's field rations, froze in the large oval-shaped pots as the fatigue parties made the long and hazardous trips to the trench line with supplies. Sickness and frost-bite took a steady toll of the men who often went a week without undressing, allowing the lice to attack in ever-increasing numbers. The trenches quickly became mud-filled, rat infested and disease ridden.

Henceforth, fighting would be of a highly diversified nature. There was nothing but desultory engagements between infantry and cavalry patrols. Apart from the weather, the task of holding the Rendina Gorge was light enough as the Bulgars had not yet crossed the frontier. Traffic through the gorge was stopped and there were patrol boats on the Lake. During most of the December period George and his mates were on one-third rations as supply ships were being regularly sunk in the Mediterranean. As this situation became acute, they scoured the area for any stray animals to get some fresh meat.

Their only comfort at this stage was the rum issue. On very cold nights they were allowed a double issue. It was in many cases a life-saver. On Christmas Day the Padre visited the various units setting up a little home made altar on a large boulder or some ammunition boxes, covered with a white cloth decked with a crucifix and a chalice. The men gathered around the altar to celebrate Mass, to hear the joyous and hopeful words of their Padre and sing some Christmas carols. No doubt George, who was still on Field Punishment, must have thought about his family back home in Moate and the many happy Christmas days he spent with them in the past.

In the New Year the Allies could carry on the work of defence under peaceful conditions, as the enemy remained inactive thirty miles away. The new defensive line became known as 'The Birdcage' or 'Birdcage Lines,' on account of the quantity of wire used. It was the last line of defence should the enemy attack and attempt to capture Salonika. The soldiers built trenches and roads, work which the troops found *tedious and unrewarding*; they also faced long hours of guard duty. While there are no soldiers that dig better than the Irish, non-hate it more so. With no enemy to attack and take their frustration out on, they tore into the countryside like demented moles on the principle of, *'if you don't like the country, dig it up!'*

To perk the men up, the food supply and the weather started to get better from January onwards. There followed a supply of corrugated iron sheets for covering their dug-outs, which much improved life on the line. By the beginning of April 1916, the experts pronounced the defensive system to be capable of prolonging resistance to the, still anxiously awaited, enemy advance. The Austrians and the Bulgarians had also fortified the heights of the hills surrounding Salonika at the same time, which would have dire consequences for the British later.

The only diversion for the force was the affair of the Kara Burun forts. They were situated at the mouth of the Vardar and were in Greek hands. The international forces under General Mahon were not too happy that the forts were seen lying in stocks of armour-piercing shells and building gun emplacements. The British, French, Italian and Russian warships in the harbour under the forts decided that enough was enough and British Marines landed, backed by French troops marched round from the city. The British Marine officer in charge of the landing party, backed by the fleet which had orders to fire if they heard gunfire, called on the first fort to surrender. As the NCO in command of the fort had only seventy men, and his officers were away on leave, he complied. The other forts seeing this followed suit. It was an extremely dangerous business, because if the Greeks had resisted, King Constantine would have used that as an excuse to bring the Germans into Greece against the Allied forces. By bluff and careful disposition of the international forces, this was averted. In February, George's Brigade was relieved by the 80th Brigade.

Following this, 29th Brigade was posted to Ajvasil, halfway to Salonika, on the shore of Lake Langaza where it was occupied in training and work on defences and roads. As Spring approached in The Birdcage, George and his infantry colleagues were smartening up their soldierly qualities again after months of digging. They carried out brigade route-matches and tactical exercises on the way. The change was most welcome after months of confinement in the narrow gullies, carving endless trenches in Salonika's stony rampart of hills.

Full-scale war on the Western Front during the period 1914-1915 proved that to be fully effective, machine-guns should be used in larger groups. It was also found that the guns, under their own commander during an operation, allowed them to be sent to areas with the greatest need. The main idea was to create specialist machine gun companies out of the machine gunners of infantry regiments. To meet this need, the Machine Gun Corps was granted a Royal Warrant on 14th October, followed by an Army Order on 22nd October 1915. As the largest group of machine gunners, the infantry machine-gun sections were the first to be transferred to the new Corps, to be formed into companies and brigades.

On 10th of May 1916, George was given a new army number of 48507 when the four Machine Gun Sections from the 6th Leinsters were transferred into the newly formed 29th Machine Company, which as the number indicated fought in support of the 29th Infantry Brigade (which included the 6th Battalion the Leinster Regiment) in the 10th Division. The battalions had lost their machine-guns to the new unit.

On the 26th May 1916 the Bulgarians invaded Greece and seized Fort Rupel, six miles across the border, compelling the garrison to leave. The following day, they occupied Fort Dragotin and Fort Kanivo, opening up the Struma valley to the enemy. Thus, any allied advance could only take place on the left flank. It later emerged that the surrender of the forts was due to a direct command from King Constantine, who received a bribe of 15,000,000 dollars from Germany.

They pushed further south occupying all of the Kavala-Drama district in Macedonia and eventually seized the Adrianople-Salonika railway, which enabled them to transport their troops and supplies. At this time Greece, the host country, was divided and still officially neutral. In the same month they attacked the British positions but were firmly repulsed. The British retaliated by triggering a series of attacks elsewhere on the front by the other Allies. Fighting went on for three days and nights in an action known as the Battle of Vardar.

The front was poorly served by the Flying Corps and George had to put up with daily attacks from the air by an enemy squadron of nineteen planes, who wrought a great deal of damage on and behind the lines. The aircraft could put the *'fear of God'* into the bravest of soldiers. I feel sure that George was no exception, as the planes and the subsequent explosions came nearer and nearer. While he must have wished to rush to his dug-out and bury himself as deep as possible until the danger had passed, he had to man his machine-gun and return fire.

During the campaign in 1916, the Serbian army was evacuated to Corfu to refit, arriving back in Salonika in May 1916. They were to be joined in July 1916 by Russian forces and in August by some Italian troops. At that time there were three French and four British Divisions in theatre, the 10th, 22nd, 26th, and the 28th. The period April to June 1916 would see a progression of these troops towards the Greek frontier, establishing forward positions which could be used for defence or offence. On 21st June 1916, the British force began to move up to the Doiran front that bridged the gap between Lake Doiran and the Vardar River.

An attempted invasion of Greece in July by the Bulgarians was repulsed near Lake Doiran. For its part, the British defensive system stood the test of the attempted invasion, but Allied pressure in the north prevented any further incursions. On 29th July the British relieved the French, who had been holding the line. Another assault in August 1916 was driven back. In counter attacks over the next few weeks British units, including the 10th Division, were engaged in capturing key features hill-top by hill-top, sending out patrols to skirmish with the enemy.

The Allied plan for the summer was to push up the river Vardar in the direction of Uskub (Skopje) in southern Serbia, but they were pre-empted by the Bulgarian-led advance from south-west Serbia into northern Greece, supported by German units. These troops inflicted a defeat on the Allies at the battle of Florina between 17th and 27th August.

In a counter-attack, Florina was recaptured. As Summer arrived they cautiously withdrew across the river Struma, but the Bulgarians did not follow.

Salonika Force spent the usually hot months of Summer 1916 still dug-in, in the Struma Valley. Here, the Bulgarian trench lines were only 1000 yards from the British, with the dominating heights of the Bulgarian strongholds seemingly impregnable. Unfortunately, summer in the central Struma Valley brought its own trials and tribulations.

George and his mates had to share their trenches with lizards, scorpions and snakes, swarming beetles, hornets, bees, and several large species of horse-fly. It was hot from March to October. At times, they were forced to march 25 miles/40 km in temperatures of 114F / 45.5C in the presence of a fine, irritating Balkan dust which got into their eyes, lungs, and hair, covering face hands and uniform with a thick layer that replaced itself as soon as it could be brushed off. Marches in this heat sometimes proved fatal. In July 1916 scores of men fainted while marching, and the intense heat rendered ammunition useless. Furthermore, warm summer nights attracted noisy swarms of the dreaded malaria-carrying mosquitoes. Against this, the soldiers were issued a muslin veil or anti-mosquito netting as protection from attacks. Worn over the head and neck it gave them some relief; however, the main protection was to take a daily five grain dose of quinine to ward off the malaria.

Added to this were these blood-sucking attacks on George's body by the 'Prussian Guard' (fleas) making him itchy to their bites. Body lice were rife in the trenches and the cause of much discomfort and it was almost impossible to get rid of them. Shaving the head and removing moustaches and beards would largely control the head lice but the body louse, that hid away in the folds, creases and pleats of their uniforms, only emerging to feed, was a far more difficult problem, particularly in cold weather when it was difficult to shed clothing. 'Crumming Up' was the soldier's slang for de-lousing, to be done as often as possible as conditions on the line permitted. Putting jam (Pozzy) on a hard-tack biscuit was a work of art as in seconds, a tasty morsel would be black with flies. George and his fellow soldiers were also open to 'Trench Mouth,' which attacked and eroded the gums, causing bleeding and ulceration. This was followed by a sloughing off of the gum membranes and particularly unpleasant breath. The ensuing pain was such that swallowing and even talking was frequently difficult. At that time and place, for every casualty of battle, three died of malaria which was endemic in the marshy river valleys along with other diseases. The troops were quoted as saying that *the weather conditions are worse than the enemy itself*.

At this stage, it was possible to evacuate the most serious cases. However, with the introduction of unrestricted submarine warfare this became no longer possible. Consequently, the cases of malaria soared as the infected men were forced to remain in Macedonia. Hospital admissions rose to 63,396 out of a strength of 100,000.

Many had numerous relapses, made worse by having to stay in the country. Even when they were finally evacuated, many would suffer relapses for years to come. In total, British forces had estimated non-battle casualties during the campaign at 505,024. However, they then went on the attack on the 17/18th August capturing Horse-shoe Hill on 18th August and already in line along the Struma River, crossing it in several places. The offensive was followed by counter attacks all in stifling hot weather with no water re-supply, in hills that were so rocky that only slit trenches could be dug. (A slit was just a shallow protective trench.) Following this, the British became solely responsible for the whole front line from the Vardar to the mouth of the Struma.

Coming out of the line was a complicated business – as when George's company would be relieved by a sister company in a night-time handover. On relief, each section would march to H.Q. to re-join their company, having handed over all tracings, defence schemes, fortnight Divisional intelligence summaries, bulk ammunition, bombs, Very lights, reserve rations and other trench stores and mutual certificates exchanged. A copy of the certificates had to be handed to Battalion H.Q. next morning. All signals stores borrowed from Division and Brigade had to be handed over intact. All moves to be carried out under cover of darkness. The mind boggles!

It was during this period that Greek Prime Minister M. Venizelos was dismissed from office and he set up an alternative government. Not until King Constantine was deposed in June 1917 was the situation resolved and Greece unified under his son Alexander and former Prime Minister Venizlos.

By September 1916, the 29th Brigade was made up of the following units: 10th (Service) Battalion The Hampshire Regiment; 6th (Service) Battalion The Royal Irish Rifles; 5th

(Service) Battalion The Connaught Rangers; 6th (Service) Battalion The Prince of Wales Leinster Regiment, and the 29th Brigade Machine Company, (George's newly formed unit).

The main allied advance against the Bulgarians finally began in that month, after the enemy had overrun eastern Macedonia. The Allies advanced north west toward Monastir in Macedonia and began pushing the Bulgarians before them. On 11th September an energetic offensive was begun along the entire front with the British, now under its new commander General G.F. Milne, crossing to the near bank of the Struma towards Serres. The success of this advance resulted in the battle honour 'Struma' being awarded to 26 infantry regiments, including those of the 10th Division. The division were manning the front line when they received an intelligence report to the effect that the railway from Doiran to Adrainople and Constantinople, which was being used by the enemy, was vulnerable where it crossed the Salonika-Seres road and the River Struma. If the Irish could capture the strategic village of Yenikoi, it would be preliminary to cutting the railway and denying it to the Bulgarians. The beginning of the operation was the capture of the villages of Karajakois and Zir during the period 30th September to 2nd October 1916. Two companies of the 6th Leinsters and six machine-guns were to be involved in the attacks. There is little doubt that George's team constituted one of the gun groups.

At 3 a.m. on the morning of the 30th they crossed the river to the enemy side and attacked. It was a complete success. The Bulgar outpost was captured before the enemy soldiers realized what was happening. However, the enemy quickly recovered and an 11 a.m. counter-attack had to be beaten off with machine-gun fire. An hour later another attack came in, this time from Yenikoi, directed at

Zir, which was checked, but not without some difficulty. The Bulgars had lost heavily in these actions

There were no more attacks after this time, but the line was shelled by enemy artillery. Twice the Bulgars entered Zir in counter-attacks but each time they were ejected, many by being bayoneted.

On 3rd October, troops of the 30th Brigade passed through the Leinsters, the Dubliners and the Royal Irish Rifles and were in possession of Yenikoi by 7.20 am. The price for the capture of the three villages was 385 men killed, wounded and missing.

11th October the Crown Prince of Serbia visited Yenikoi and congratulated the Irish troops on their advance. By the middle of October, the British were hammering at the Seres fortress. The campaign was successful with the capture of the hated Fort Rupel and the Rupel Pass, with advances being made to within a few miles of Serres. In Macedonia, so rapid had been the advance by the Allies that the Bulgarians were forced to abandon their entire line of frontier defences centred on Kneali, and retreat across the Viro and Bistritza Rivers toward Monastir on the west side. After a four-day fight and fearing the loss of their entire army, the Bulgarians and Germans evacuated Monastir on the night of 18th November 1916, retreating northwards. Meanwhile on the right of the Allied line, between Vardar and Doiran, the Bulgarians had shown strong resistance.

As Allied troops advanced in November, Monastir fell and it was at this time that the temperature started to fall. In the inhospitable mountainous terrain and adverse weather conditions, ice and snow in the winter, the enemy used the cover of the blizzards to attack the British lines. In attacks where the bayonet was used, men bled to death, their bodies being buried behind the trench line in what the soldiers called 'Stiff's Paddock' (temporary burial ground). The battle ground was terribly rocky and splinters created by shellfire killed or wounded many of them. This was misery and torment that George and his mates were confined to as they settled down to the brutal and static trench war of attrition. The dug-out where the machine-gunners and the bombers lived was called Suicide Annex, and the group were known as the Suicide Club.

A machine-gunner could lay down enough fire to kill or injure a battalion of enemy soldiers, who were generally executed if captured as they caused so much death and injury.

The Brigade spent their second Christmas (1916) in relative peace and for the first-time George could enjoy all the trappings of plum puddings from England and local turkeys, with rum punch and some element of entertainment. The weather was back to freezing cold, with heavy snowfalls and much flooding. It was impossible to remove the snow and water from the trenches in daylight and this work had to be done at night, thus leaving the defenders up to their knees in slush and water during daylight hours. However, the troops were better clothed and equipped to deal with it than they were the last winter. Irish patrols, when they could operate through the snowdrifts encountered little resistance as it appeared that the bulk of the enemy had pulled out of the valley, which was now held by a small rear-guard.

CHAPTER 9

THE EASTER UPRISING

Depend upon it that lovers of freedom will be free.

(Edmund Burke)

Back in Ireland a hardcore of Irish Volunteers and Irish Republican Brotherhood members, who had voted against joining the British army and going to war, reasoned that with the vast majority of British soldiers tied down in an escalating war, they could exploit the situation for Ireland's freedom. So, planning began for an uprising in 1916. Thomas Clarke was the main instigator of the rising along with Eamonn Ceannt, Sean Mac Diarmada, Sean T. O Ceallaigh and Padraig H. Pearse. They were later joined by James Connolly, Thomas McDonagh and Joseph Plunket. Connolly issued a call to arms in his paper 'The Workers Republic'. Both Connolly's Citizens Army and the Irish Volunteers held recruitment meetings throughout Ireland and stepped up their training.

The rising was set for Easter Saturday, 22nd April 1916. However, some significant setbacks occurred which included the capture of Sir Roger Casement after he was put ashore from a German submarine at Banna Strand in Tralee Bay, Co. Kerry. The weapons he had procured from the Germans were lost when they were intercepted by the Royal Navy. In the meantime, the plans for the rising were discovered by the British during a raid on German officials in New York.

It was unanimously decided to carry on, although it had little or no chance of success. On Easter Monday 24th April 1916, the General Post Office in Dublin City centre was taken over by the revolutionary forces, where Padraig Pearse read out the following Proclamation of the Republic to a gathering crowd:

POBLACHT NA EIREANN
THE PROVISIONAL GOVERNMENT OF THE IRISH REPUBLIC TO
THE PEOPLE OF IRELAND

'IRISHMEN AND WOMEN: In the name of God and of the dead generations from which she receives her old tradition of nationhood, Ireland, through us, summons her children to her flag and strikes for her freedom

Having organised and trained her manhood through her secret revolutionary organisation, the Irish Republican Brotherhood, and through her other military organisations, the Irish Volunteers and the Irish Citizen Army, having patiently perfected her discipline, having resolutely waited for the right moment to reveal itself, she now seizes that moment, and supported by her exiled children in America and by gallant allies in Europe, but relying in the first on her own strength, she strikes in full confidence of victory.

We declare the right of the people of Ireland to the ownership of Ireland, and to the unfettered control of Irish destinies, to be sovereign and indefeasible. The long usurpation of that right by a foreign people and government has not extinguished the right, nor can it ever be extinguished except by the destruction of the Irish people. In every generation the Irish people have asserted their right to national freedom and sovereignty six times during *the past three hundred years they have asserted it in arms. Standing on that fundamental right and again asserting it in arms in the face of the world, we hereby proclaim the Irish Republic as a sovereign Independent State, and we pledge our lives and the lives of our comrades-in-arms to the cause of its freedom, of its welfare, and of its exaltation among the nations.*

The Irish Republic is entitled to, and hereby claims, the allegiance of every Irishman and Irishwoman. The Republic guarantees religious and civil liberty, equal rights and equal opportunities to all its citizens, and declares its resolve to pursue the happiness and prosperity of the whole nation and of all parts, cherishing all the children of the nation equally, and oblivious of the differences carefully fostered by an alien government, which have divided a minority from the majority in the past.

Until our arms have brought the opportune moment for the establishment of a permanent National Government, representative of the whole people of Ireland and elected by the suffrages of all her men and women, the Provisional Government, hereby constituted, will administer the civil and military affairs of the Republic in trust for the people. We place the cause of the Irish Republic under the protection of the Most High God, Whose blessing we invoke upon our arms, and we pray that no one who serves the cause will dishonour it by cowardice, inhumanity, or rapine. In this supreme hour the Irish nation must, by its valour and discipline and by readiness of its children to sacrifice themselves for the common good, prove itself worthy of the august destiny to which it is called.'

Signed by the leaders of the Rising: Thomas J. Clarke, Eamonn Ceannt, James Connolly, Thomas MacDonagh, Sean Mac Diarmada, P.H. Pearse and Joseph Plunkett, and promulgated on Easter Sunday, 23rd April 1916 at Liberty Hall Dublin.

The Rebels fortified the General Post Office in the city centre and other points around the city. The raising of the green flag with the words 'Irish Republic' written across it, along with a green, white and orange tricolour (which was actually supposed to be the flag of 'E Company' in the Post Office and not of the Republic, though it later came to be identified with the Republic). Along with the readings of the Proclamation of Independence were to threaten a bloody war. Five other positions were seized and fortified; Boland's Mill, the Four Courts, Jacobs Factory, St. Stephan's Green and the South Dublin Union.

The rest of the country failed to rise, leaving the insurgents in Dublin alone and isolated. By Wednesday the revolutionaries, 1,000 Irish Volunteers and 200 members of the Citizen Army were outnumbered 20 to 1, facing fire from machine-guns, artillery shells and naval guns from the *Helga*, a British Navy gunboat. By Friday the GPO was engulfed in flame. With the death toll mounting and being critically short of ammunition and food, capitulation became inevitable. In a final communiqué to his men, Commander-in-Chief Padraig Pearse wrote:

> *'I desire now, lest I may not have an opportunity later, to pay homage to the gallantry of the soldiers of Irish Freedom who have during the past four days been writing with fire and steel the most glorious chapter in the later history of Ireland. Justice can never be done to their heroism, to the discipline, to their gay and unconquerable spirit in the midst of peril and death.'*

Then he gave the order to surrender. This led to 3,000 people being arrested, with 1,841 of them interned without trial in internment camps in Ballykinlar in the parish of Tyrella near Downpatrick in County Down, Northern Ireland, The Curragh Camp in County Kildare and Frongoch near Bala, North Wales, under the Defence of the Realm Act 1914.

Of these, 171 were tried by a secret court martial with 170 convictions, 90 of whom were sentenced to death of which 75 were commuted to life imprisonment. Over the following weeks and in a colossal misreading of the Irish public, the English executed the seven signatories to the proclamation and leaders of the rising.

The executions gained the rebel cause the full backing of the people, in recognition of the sheer courage of what the rebels had attempted to achieve. This marked a crucial turning on the path to attaining self-government. The Rising put an end to the democratic constitutional and conciliatory parliamentary movement and replaced it with a radical physical-force approach. Over 400 people died in the Rising.

People of Westmeath regarded the arrests of people in Athlone following the Easter Rising as unjust, as they had not engaged in any violent activity. This was to have significance in time to come.

Savage repression that followed the Rising stimulated militarism among nationalists, including those who had advocated peaceful parliamentary protests. The Rising was critical in terms of the overall fight for the Irish Republic. For the first time, the mass of the Irish people wanted an end to English rule, and Nationalism swept the country. These realisations were in all probabilities the main aim of the insurgents. The War of Independence which followed in 1919, the ensuing Civil War and the formation of the Irish Free State can be traced back to the Easter Rising. Its influence was to play a vital part in the life of George Adamson.

Survivors of the Easter Rebellion such as Cathal Brugha,

Michael Collins, Richard Mulcahy and Eamon de Valera established their supremacy in rebuilding The Irish Republican Brotherhood, The Irish Citizen Army, Fianna Eireann, Hibernian Rifles, Fianna Eireann and the Irish Volunteers, decimated in the Easter Rising. Eamon de Valera would eventually take over leadership of Sinn Fein (We Ourselves).

There are numerous records of Irish soldiers' opinions in the war zones of the Great War with regard to the general political situation in Britain at the time. However, little is known of the opinion of the soldiers of the Irish regiments in Salonika, regarding the Easter Rising. This may be because the news was censored in order to keep up morale, added to the fact that the men had no home leave. So, to soldiers of the 10th Irish Division like George, little or no news came through from Ireland. It didn't help that letters arrived on an ad hoc-basis, marked salvaged from the sea, where ships had been holed or sunk by enemy action. Sometimes, the post was dumped as there was no transport available to deliver it, or it never came at all.

It was a different story in India some three and half years later, where on June 28th 1920, the 1st Battalion the Connaught Rangers on garrison duty in Jullunder, heard the news of the Black and Tan atrocities at home. It led to a mutiny in the ranks, led by James Daly from Tyrrellspass, County Westmeath. This resulted in Daly's court-martial and subsequent execution on July 2nd 1920.

CHAPTER 10

If you're going through hell, keep going.

(Winston Churchill)

Major attacks by the 10th Division, which included the 29th Brigade, carried on to mid-November when operations in the Sturma valley became impossible due to the approach of winter. In the rainy weather, the ground would be reduced to a sea of mud. The clouds piled up looking like mighty mountains in the blue of the lightning strikes. Rain sheeted down in a slanting curtain, cutting through even the strongest of temporary cover. The thunderstorms badly affected the soldiers who were not used to them; it tortured their eardrums as they stood in the trenches. Casualties from disease were sometimes 100% of the strength of some units present and at other times, caused ten casualties for every one inflicted by the enemy. At one time, the troops were attacked by a severe epidemic of flu that laid men low and resultantly having to be withdrawn from the front. The afflicted soldiers lay helpless for days with bodies trembling and wanting neither food nor drink. Some lost all desire to live. Most recovered within a fortnight and were returned to the lines.

At this time, George's home from home was the ubiquitous trench, which is in essence an elongated grave, deep and narrow, so that two men could hardly pass each other in the confined space. It was part of a complicated system of interlinking lines of trenches.

The communications trenches were at a right angle with the front-line ones, and from one to the other were turnings and angles leading to rest and dug-outs. At times in a successful counter attack, they could become veritable slaughter houses. The conditions in them were appalling.

During the winter months they were constantly filled with mud and water, blood, body parts, faeces and urine. George had no choice but to stand in these conditions day and night. As the best protection from getting 'Trench Foot' he was told to keep his feet dry; he was ordered to carry extra socks, wash his feet daily, apply whale oil and change his socks. He was advised to keep his wet socks against his body to dry them out. In essence, most soldiers failed to do this because of the intense conditions and the indisputable fact they never had the energy or the time. The virtual immobility of George and his mates in the trenches meant they were forced to spend long hours with their feet exposed to the wet and cold.

The British Army ammunition boot was made of leather and not effectively waterproof. After some hours, or days of exposure, the soldier's feet were waterlogged and chilled. If these conditions continued, the skin began to break down. They became swollen, blisters formed and eventually became numb from nerve damage. Over time, they could also become infected by a fungus. If the situation wasn't quickly resolved by drying the skin and getting circulation re-established, gangrene could ensue. In the worst cases, amputation became necessary.

At this stage, the British could only undertake raids and lay down 'Chinese Barrages', a bombardment to deceive the Bulgarians into believing that a large-scale assault was planned, to prevent movement by them. The only real activity in the sector was time spent on raids. Unfortunately, this type of action could turn out to be extremely costly, with night patrols from each side trying to ambush the other. Many men died or were wounded in this low-level fighting, which took place mainly outside the front line trenches. In the Bulgarian attacks, enemy soldiers came on blowing bugles and shouting 'Allah'. George and his fellow machine-gunners caught them in the open, stopping them dead in their tracks. Trench raids were carried out by the British, with an eight or ten man squad, each carrying two Mills bombs, rifle grenades and trench mortars in their haversack. They would creep up to the Bulgarian trench line and lob their bombs into their trenches. The trip out, along precipitous and sharply looping mountain tracks was terribly slow and hazardous in the extreme. The return from such a raid was doubly hazardous, as the attack would turn the Bulgarian positions into a hornet's nest of retaliation, with machine gun and artillery peppering no-man's land and making the return journey exceedingly unpleasant indeed. To George, the sound of the bullets as they passed overhead was like being in a heavy thunderstorm, only this one was lethal. It was a case of 'shoot and scoot'. In these actions, George had to cope with the suddenness of death and the grief at the loss of a friend, who went out into the night with him, never to return. Plus, the chances of getting a badly wounded comrade back were very small. Active patrolling went on both day and night.

CHAPTER 11

Tough times never last, but tough people do.

(Robert Shull)

Front-line duty for George during these times also consisted of being a member of a 'Black Hand Gang' (a trench raiding party) or of a 'Silent Death' detail, waiting quietly at night in a no man's land for the advent of a Bulgarian patrol. The enemy was then dispatched hand-to-hand, as quickly as possible by the use of a 'Tin Opener' (a bayonet). Fighting with the bayonet was particularly scary. It was no fun being out in front of the company lines and open to attack by raiding parties of Bulgarians who knew every inch of the ground. Throughout the campaign that followed, the main function of British forces on the right of the Allied line, was to mount local attacks to prevent Bulgarian troops being diverted to key operations on the left flank. The position along the front became a war of attrition.

During this period, working and fatigue parties were made up of poor souls such as George, who 'Drew Crabs' (attracted enemy shellfire) in sporadic bursts as they moved about carrying ammunition to the trenches. A night time duty would entail being a member of a wiring party, where barbed wire was placed in front of the trenches to make it difficult for enemy soldiers to get into the trench line. Unfortunately, the noise of hammering the fixing stakes into the ground attracted enemy fire, despite the fact that the Irish muffled their stake pickets with blankets. This was another suicide type job which was alleviated when the army started to issue the 'Corkscrew', or Iron Screw Picket, a looped steel post, for staking the barbed wire. The corkscrew end enabled the stake to be twisted quietly into the ground without alerting the enemy. This type of duty often left men 'On the Wire' (missing or killed in action).

Digging in the frozen ground was a dangerous, heavy and onerous task, which could be interrupted by night attacks, machine-gun fire or enemy bombardments by trench mortars and heavy artillery. On top of all this, George still had to get some 'Kipp' (sleep). This was very difficult for him, as his two hours on 'Stag' (sentry duty) followed by four hours rest, was interrupted by intermittent bombardment.

This shelling, called 'Brock's Benefit' (after the well-known-firework manufacturer) came from major artillery positions occupied by the Bulgarians, covering the Greek valley of the Struma River and Serres. These guns inflicted George and his mates with the dawn 'Hate' (bombardment) – the sudden boom of a gun, then a roar like the sound of an approaching train, coming nearer and nearer, the rattling scream of the shell rising to a high demonic shriek as it closed on its target, its fearful crescendo enough to wake the dead. A moment later a sheet of lurid flame leapt from the site of the impact, and the thunder would echo endlessly down the trench line. There was a shuddering compression as the ground quaked and trembled. It was like being inside a big bell that had just struck. It sucked the air from the lungs, and the following blast of hot air could incinerate any animal or human caught in its blast. Being too close to a shell-burst when it blasted out, then back in, could burn George's lungs and turn his organs into soup.

In a direct hit, the forces of the explosion would take the line of least resistance to escape the confines of the trench, surging through the trench, destroying everything in its path, blowing its occupants apart, making the remains of the trench look like the inside of a butcher's shop. The Germans fired shrapnel shells that burst with a cloud-like explosion. The shrapnel from this type of shelling was worse than a bullet. A bullet wound was clean, but shrapnel could tear a man to pieces. All this was topped and tailed by 'Stand To' (state of alert in the trenches at dawn, or dusk when enemy attack was most likely). At this time, it was the height of winter, a man's feet froze solid in his 'Ammo Boots' (from ammunition boots, regulation issue hob nailed boots). On the order 'Stand Down' George and the boys were given an issue of rum, followed by a breakfast of tea, bacon and bread. Then, except for the sentries, the off-duty lads retired to their small dug-outs which were capable of housing three of four soldiers, and got their 'heads down'. In the main George's days were made up of drills, work, sentry and outpost duty, and fatigues with on occasion football and recreation.

Most nights would have its burial fatigue, where George could be detailed off to dig a pit to bury the dead of the previous day's bombardments and patrols. Digging in the frozen ground was another very dangerous, onerous and heavy task which could be interrupted by night attacks, machine-gun fire or enemy bombardments. For a short time George's thoughts might have been diverted by the beauty of a star-filled night sky, or the rising of a full moon above the rugged landscape, until a 'strafe' of guns along the distant hills and a Very light or two reminded him of his present position in the scheme of things.

The 29th Brigade, would spend 44 days in the line, then have a two-week break in a camp, situated behind the lines in a secure area. In the rest camp George would have slept in a two-man bivouac, which consisted of two waterproof ground-sheets with various buttons around the borders. When buttoned together they made a six foot, two-man tent. The tent was supported by a four-foot stick at either end and was pegged into the ground through special eyelets.

This contraption was nothing less than an open-ended wind tunnel. George would have used his back-pack, webbing and any spare kit to block up one end of the 'bivvi'. His flimsy shelter was liable to collapse in the dead of the night or in the middle of a thunderstorm. These rest camps, situated in ravines safe from enemy artillery observers, were at times washed away by melted snow and heavy rain, turning small streams into raging rivers.

It appears that some of the rank and file were given time off to visit and explore the city of Salonika. Some poor souls had never been to Salonika in over two years. George did in fact do so, as he bought and brought home some souvenir hankies for his mother and his sisters. He was able to enter music halls if he chose, where there was bad dancing, bad singing and bad beer all at extortionate prices. Most of the soldiers spent any leave time they could get in the YMCA and E.F. canteens. He would have found the city to be a foul, dirty place, the dirt and squalor accounting for much fever. Though he longed for some respite, it was little recompense for the months spent amidst sweltering, rocky ravines and shrapnel haunted trenches, watching his wounded or fever-stricken friends dwindle away one by one. It was remarked by an officer that the cheerfulness of the Irish soldiers in the face of countless drawbacks was truly remarkable.

During 1917, once again there was comparatively little activity on the British part of the front in Macedonia, due in part to complex political changes in Greece throughout the year. The stalemate allowed the Irish of the 10th Division to celebrate on 17th of March (St. Patrick's Day). When after an-open air Mass by the Catholic Padre Father Rusher and an afternoon of sports, the Irish went about the 'wetting of St. Patrick's head.'

'Not a dozen, sober men in camp could be seen.'

It was a welcome break from the horrors of war for George and the rest of the Irish contingent, although one Irish soldier was reported to have died from alcohol poisoning. (The camp in question appears to have been Camp Langavuk.)

With St. Patrick duly celebrated the 10th Division were back in the thick of it again. The main fighting took place around Lake Doiran, where the line was adjusted several times by each side early in the year. In April 1917 the British attacked, gaining a considerable amount of ground and resisting strong counter-attacks.

In May, the Bulgarians attacked the British positions but were firmly repulsed. On 24th April, and again in May 1917 British attacks against the Bulgarian trenches at Doiran were beaten back with heavy losses from Bulgarian artillery and machine guns. On 28th April 1917, an outpost on the left bank of Belica was raided by the enemy. The Bulgars, about forty strong, crawled up through the long grass and threw in a shower of bombs. The post withdrew in excellent order, losing two men. The next day a raid took place to feel the strength of the Bulgars in and around Kjupri, supported by two Vickers machine-guns. The raiders established that the garrison of the village consisted of about sixty or seventy men.

The 29th Brigade was to make an attack and hold the ground won. The most crucial tasks were given to the 6th Irish Rifles, who were to capture the village of Kjupri, and the 6th Leinsters who were to attack their left. The attack was carried out on 7th May, but of the assault itself there is no official record. All the objectives were attained. The Bulgarian artillery shelled the Irish all night, with the intensity of the barrage increasing at 3.30 a.m. At 5 a.m, the enemy attacked and were stopped by a Lewis machine gun in the post. At 6 a.m, there was another attack, also dominated by the Lewis gun and rifle fire. At 6.45 a very powerful enemy force attacked, but the return fire took a considerable number of the enemy, and the artillery finished the job. A fine patrol by the 6th Leinsters was fought at this time, which resulted in the capture of about a dozen Bulgars and, more importantly, a German non-commissioned officer. The German had in his possession a number of clips of ammunition with the bullets reversed. Such a bullet would make a hole in a man one could put a fist through. It was noted, and the said German's confinement was not passed in the most pleasant of conditions.

CHAPTER 12

War is a series of catastrophes that results in a victory

(Georges Clemenceau)

British action in May triggered a series of attacks elsewhere on the front. The actions came to be known as the Battle of Vardar. In that year, the British line extended from the mouth of the Sturma River at the Gulf of Orfano, past Lakes Thinoa, Butkovs and Doiran to the Vardar River. At the end of May, it was decided that the unhealthy valley of the Struma should be evacuated for the hot months in order to avoid the risk of another serious malaria epidemic. By the night of 5th June, the Struma valley was clear, the last outpost moving up the slopes in the early morning of the 7th. It also began to appear as though the Bulgars, though more used to this sort of climate than the British, had evacuated the valley of the Struma, leaving no more than a screen of troops in it.

Meanwhile, on 27th June 1917, General Allenby, formally commander of the British Third Army in France, was made commander-in-chief of the British Expeditionary Force in Egypt, with orders to take the war in that area to the Turks in Palestine. Having studied his new command, he decided he needed reinforcements if he was to reach Jerusalem and he was promised the 10th (Irish) Division.

The 10th spent the August period in intensive training, which was brought to a sudden halt by orders for a move to Palestine. The

Division was ordered to concentrate at the main base on the Seres-Salonika road. Here re-equipping was hastily carried out ready for embarkation. So, on 12th September 1917, George paraded in 'Christmas Tree Order' (parading in full equipment with all his kit).

His clothing issue consisted of a peaked cap, a jacket with patch pockets, trousers with putties and ankle boots. He carried a spare pair of boots, a spare suit of the service dress, including the peak cap and a spare set of underwear, all stored in his Kitbag. The Kitbag was left at base camp in the care of the company store man. He also had with him a spare pair of socks and a knitted woollen head-dress known as a 'cap comforter' and a greatcoat. He carried his steel helmet, which in 1915 was initially the only Trench Stores item used in turn by troops in the line. It was primarily aimed at protection from shrapnel, but it offered only limited protection against a direct hit by rifle or machine-gun fire. In 1916, it became the standard issue.

His equipment, apart from his revolver, consisted of the 1908 pattern webbing, which was made up of a three-inch wide belt and two shoulder braces, vertically in front and over the back like an ordinary pair of a man's braces. Both belt and braces were fitted with various buckles and end-tags so they could be fitted together in several different ways.

Attached to the webbing were a pair of ammunition carriers, each carrying 75 rounds, a haversack worn on the left hip, a bayonet frog complete with bayonet worn on the left side of the belt, a water bottle worn in a sling on the right hip. He also carried an entrenching tool, which was a combination pick and shovel. The pack worn on his back contained his greatcoat, mess tin, washing kit, some spare clothing and a groundsheet. All this had a total weight of 61.lbs / 28 Kg. If the back pack were discarded, an extra 100 rounds of ammunition was carried. It was often said that the definition of a soldier was 'somebody to hang things on'.

The High Command did not wish the Allies to realize that large bodies of troops were leaving Salonika, so embarkation was to take place very quietly at night. On 12th September 1917 George, after two years of bitter fighting in the Balkans, embarked on a troopship but remained for two days on board in the harbour, waiting for two destroyer escorts.

Then, along with the rest of the 10th Division he set sail for the Egyptian theatre of war. The voyage was through the blue waters of the Aegean with a stop at Skiros where the troops bathed, then on through the grey, green Mediterranean. The entire voyage, except for new sights and sounds, was uneventful.[2]

---

[2] On 18th August 1918, before the conclusion of the war in Salonika, (an Armistice was finally signed on 30th September 1918 when hostilities came to a close) the 10th (Irish) Division was awarded the campaign honour 'Macedonia 1915-1918'. The Bulgarian army lost an estimated 90,000 troops during the conflict.

CHAPTER 13

PALESTINE

The greater the difficulty, the more the glory in surmounting it.

(Epicurus)

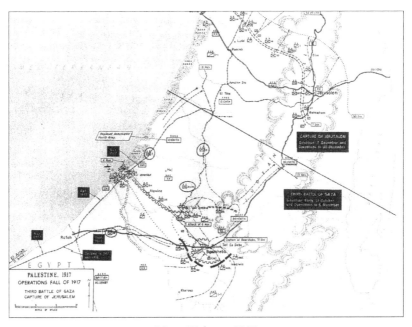

Map of Palestine 1917

George's first sights of Egypt were the desert, the Napoleonic forts of Aboukir Bay and the port of Alexandria where he disembarked on the 28th September 1917. Even after Salonika the heat was terrific. He would have marched in the unrelenting and baking sun followed by a rabble offering everything from Egyptian trinkets to fruit, all in a smattering of languages and dialects, to the railway to board a train for Moascar; then on past the massive Roman theatre that Napoleon Bonaparte's legions had discovered while digging to create new fortifications, the dig site known as The Kom Al-Dikka.

Division went into camp at Kantara, which by now was an exceptionally large base, virtually a canvas city with well-marked roads and huge dumps of ammunition and stores. Following re-assembly there and new kit issues (Tropical light-weights), they were inspected by General Lord Edmund Henry Hynman Allenby (nicknamed The Bull), Commander-in Chief of the Egyptian Expeditionary Force (EEF), their new C.O. After a successful parade and inspection, the 10th Division were posted to 20th Corps.

George and his mates moved on to the Kantara rail-head. From there they were transported by train along a single-line railway laid by the Royal Engineers. The open box cars, with up to thirty troops to a wagon made a journey of some 300 km across the Sinai desert.

In line with the railway, the Engineers had laid a large pipe across the desert to carry Nile water to the front. George's journey took him through Katia bir el Abd and along the ancient caravan route through Bir el Mazar, Badaweel to El Arish. A tiresome trip was made in cramped and boiling conditions, and Rafa, his destination couldn't come soon enough. After a full day's rest, he and his comrades finally arrived at Rafa. Reassembled on 16th October 1917 the 10th (Irish) Division joined General Chetwode's 20th Corps as part of the Egyptian Expeditionary Force.

At the outbreak of the Great War, the British government realised that it had to keep the Suez Canal open as it was the main sea route to its eastern colonies. Suez, a nominal Turkish province, bordered Egypt. When Turkey sided with Germany against Britain in 1915, it attacked the Suez Canal. Following this, Britain declared war on Turkey and began offensive action against its armed forces in the area. The Sinai and Palestine Campaign which followed was a series of battles which took place on the Sinai Peninsula, Palestine and Syria, between 28th January 1915 and 28th October 1918 when British, Indian, Australian and New Zealand troops opposed German and Turkish forces.

In 1917 The British army in Egypt was ordered to go on the offensive against the Ottoman Turks in Palestine. At this time, the Turks were holding a rough line from the fort at Gaza on the shore of the Mediterranean Sea, to the town of Beersheba which was the terminus of the Turkish railway that extended north to Damascus. Opposing the British in Gaza were the Seventh and Eight Armies, which operated in Southern Palestine and contained nine infantry divisions and one cavalry division, some 35,000 men holding a supremely defensible position. The Turkish soldier was a fearless, tough, professional fighting man who always fought hard to hold such positions and tended to go on fighting until killed, wounded or overrun.

By 1917 significant changes had taken place in the Ottoman army. The Germans formed a special task force code named "Jilderim" under the command of General Erich Von Falkenhayn. In 1913, Falkenhayn held the position of Prussian Minister of War, becoming chief of the General Staff of the German Army in 1914. He was replaced by Hindenburg after Verdun in 1916 when he took military command of Turkish-Palestine.

A seasoned soldier and commander, he reorganized the Turkish forces under the leadership of senior German officers. Prior to the arrival of the Irish, British troops had fought their way the 90 miles north to Rafa which they captured in January 1917, placing them some 30 miles from the enemy forces in Gaza. Since January 1916 the Egyptian Expeditionary Force had pushed across the Sinai desert, constructing a railway and a freshwater pipeline from the Suez Canal to maintain a base of operations on the southern border of Palestine, south of Gaza. From this, two attempts were made to capture Gaza. One on 26th March, the First Battle of Gaza, and then, on 19th April 1916, the Second Battle of Gaza. Both ended in costly failures leaving the two sides at a stalemate.

This was to change with the appointment of General Allenby as the force's new commander. While the previous commander of British Forces conducted operations from The Savoy Hotel in Cairo, Allenby moved his H.Q. to the desert itself, riding among his troops with only an orderly instead of the usual retinue of thirty or more staff officers. By October 1917 the British under Allenby was ready to strike again. Thus, having been in theatre since September 1917 and under his new Commander in Chief, battalion machine gunner George Adamson took part in the Third Battle of Gaza.

Southern Palestine, the new ground George was to fight over was not the land of milk and honey which any biblical student might have expected to find. It was stony, hilly and almost waterless in summer, with some of the most unforgiving, vast tracts of uninhabited open areas and sparse landscape in the world. Heat coming up from the sand could crack the soles of his ammo boots. His steel helmet made him feel as if his head were being poached. He also had to contend with an unquenchable thirst, compounded by an appalling shortage of drinking water. An issue of only three pints had to last him for forty-eight hours in the waterless wilderness that made up the bulk of Palestinian territory.

Temperature was raging hot during the day, between 110F / 43.3C and 130F / 54.4C with excessive humidity, leaving George and his mates without energy to do anything. This was followed by the bitter cold of the frigid nights, with its only consolation being the beautiful star filled night sky. The Turks were not the only enemy George had to contend with. He could well have believed that the 'The Prussian Guard' had followed him from Greece, as malaria-bearing mosquitoes came back to haunt, taunt and torture him, along with six-inch-long centipedes, scorpions and enormous black spiders.

Swarms of tiny sand flies were the worst; they not only extracted blood but also laid eggs in his skin, adding to his turmoil and nearly driving him crazy at times. He may well have reflected that the lice had travelled with him from Salonika as along with the sand flies, they happily reproduced in every nook and cranny of his body. George and the rest of the 10th Division men, it was noticed, were acutely fatigued even after short marches. They had not fully recovered from the dysentery and malaria in the Struma valley. Then there was the sand, blowing clouds of dust that almost suffocated him. It got everywhere, in his eyes, ears, nose and mouth and every piece of food he tried to eat. It got into his revolver, his personal weapon, fouling it greatly. His main weapon and his *raison d'être* as a machine gunner, his machine gun fared even worse, especially when it was windy. This led to a constant battle to keep his weapons in working order. But he was to find that if he kept his weapons lightly oiled the sand was not a major problem. In general, his life and the lives of his crew and the 29th Brigade infantrymen depended on his gun being in working order at all times.

The action from this day forward would be through fortified defensive lines, based on key strategic towns and, at times back to the trench warfare and night time fighting patrols that George experienced in Greece and Serbia. It was to become open warfare, as against the trench warfare in Salonika. Initially, the Irish Division was given the task of covering the completion of the railway construction as far as Karm during the build-up and deployment of the British Forces, pending attack. In order to capture Jerusalem, Allenby needed to break the enemy defences at Gaza-Beersheba where they were entrenched along a 40 km line, with special fortifications and trench systems at Gaza, Es Sheria and Beersheba. The success of the push to take Gaza hinged on the capture of Beersheba, which was the responsibility of 20th Corps. Beersheba was a small town situated on the north bank of the Wadi es-Saba. With five main roads emanating from it in all directions, the terminus for a narrow-gauge railway and its numerous wells was a prime objective for the EEF.

Mobility in this theatre was essential and to assist in this, small arms ammunition pack mules were re-equipped to carry machine-guns. Preparations for the advance took place in a sandstorm, which lasted three days. George and his team worked in preparation with goggles covering their eyes and handkerchiefs over their nose and mouth, George making good use of the souvenir hankies he bought in Salonika.

On 27th October the Third Battle of Gaza began. From the 28th to the 31st, three British divisions and 218 artillery guns bombarded the enemy garrison in Gaza but when the attack went in on the 31st October it was on Beersheba, to the east of Gaza. It was a ploy to fool the Turks into believing that a full-frontal assault on Gaza was imminent.

In one of the most remarkable feats of planning and execution, the British were able to move some 40,000 men and a similar number of horses over hostile and inhospitable terrain to Beersheba, without being detected by the enemy. In the first phase of the infantry assault, three British brigades attacked on 31st October supported by counter-battery work against the Austrian and Turkish guns that supported the Turks. The attack went without a hitch. The Australians of the Desert Mounted Corps charged across four miles of open terrain, through machine gun and artillery fire to capture the Turkish outposts to the east of Beersheba. Thus fell the ancient city of Beersheba with thousands of prisoners and artillery pieces captured. The battlefields were strewn with at least a thousand Turkish dead.

The 10th (Irish) Division were expected to cross the Wadi es-Saba on 4th November and go west towards a strong Turkish defence system called the Khawukah/Rushdi, but due to a *khamsin* (wind) which blew for two days they were not in the position until the 6th. They were tasked with taking the Hureyra Redoubt, one of the most heavily fortified of the Turkish defensive positions. To reach the objective the Irish had to cross a flat, open plain swept by machine-gun and rifle fire. They were well supported by the likes of George and his fellow machine gunners, and it was finally captured after three hours of heavy fighting.

Following this defeat, the Turks retreated from Beersheba in excellent order to pre-prepared defensive positions. For the Allies, the following days were spent fighting a difficult and bloody battle at Tel el Khuweilfe to the north west. As Allenby struck, the enemy evacuated Gaza to avoid the trap, only to be pursued. His well-planned and executed attack broke the Turkish defences leaving both Turkish Armies retreating up the coast to Jerusalem.

As George and his fellow gunners hurried through a deserted Gaza, they found it covered with the debris of war and enshrouded in a thick black cloud of smoke. From that day onwards the enemy was in flight. On the 13th Allenby, closely pursuing the Turks, struck again, driving them north and turning them towards Jerusalem.

Allenby's new tactics were not to give the enemy time to dig in. So for George and 10th, the war became one of movement following the highly visible enemy. This entailed long marches through the steep and winding ravines, stony valleys, up and over tumultuous hills. The stones were everywhere, ranging from pebbles to giant boulders. This rocky, boulder strewn ground was often precipitous and extremely slippery after rain. To George, the Judean foothills were a real hell. Moreover, through this he and his crew had to transport the machine-gun and all the other heavy paraphernalia over this pitiless terrain – in one murderous trek.

George's Brigade made a march of 12 miles in a terrific thunderstorm which continued through the night, making the earth run with water and a custard-like mud. All this in the non-stop rain, with George and his fellows dressed in shorts and pith helmets with no greatcoats, their boots letting in water and the mud clinging to everything. They had to bivouac and try to sleep in the sluicing rain with their blankets soaking wet and covered with the mud, which underfoot was sometimes eight inches deep.

Shaken out of a fitful, interrupted sleep they marched on, with much of the going up hills covered with boulders and rocks, with their feet covered in blisters. Tortured by flies, thirst and sandstorms, in clothes they hadn't changed for days until they were caked as hard as a board with sand and sweat and often on half rations, they pushed the enemy back. It added to their discomfort that there was an absence of proper shelter from the changing temperatures day and night. At this stage, a day's rations were two cups of cocoa, a bit of cheese, a few biscuits and dates when available. Some days George had to go without a meal of any kind.

There were no facilities for washing and at times he hadn't had a wash for days, forcing him to grow a beard again. As there were no replacements for boots and clothing, his uniform was tattered, dirty and blood-stained. Practically all the men wore bandages around bloody knees, where their bare knees had been cut by rocks, leading to septic sores. All the men were terribly thin and wretched looking. Their cheek bones stood out prominently, dark rings under their eyes from many sleepless nights and countless privations. Rest periods were marked by boredom, discomfort and monotony. Any leave was out of the question. Everywhere they encountered the debris of war, with dead Turks, dead camels, mules and horses. After a couple of days the dead were turning black and green, their bellies swollen, the smells dreadful. To make matters worse, a terrible *khamsin*, blowing like a blast furnace, scorched skin into sores and dried parched, thirsting throats. Feet suffered considerably, with the uppers of boots cut and slashed on sharp stones.

The prize for Allenby, George and the Expeditionary Force was now Jerusalem. When the Turkish position of Wadi Sarar fell to a British attack, the German General tried to stop the British advance on a defensive line running from Bethlehem through Jerusalem to Jaffa. On the 14th the vital point of Junction Station, twenty miles west of Jerusalem, was taken and on 17th Jaffa fell.

The Turkish army was cut in two, one half retreating eastwards, the other northward. During 7th and 9th December, the 10th Irish Division participated in General Allenby's capture of Jerusalem, as on Sunday morning 9th December the Turks vacated the Holy City. After four centuries, the Turk was leaving the land of his presence in the bitterness of defeat. They retreated north to take up defensive positions in and around Nablus. In this action and the rout that followed, twelve thousand prisoners were taken.

Two days later, on 10th December 1917 Jerusalem surrendered to the British. General Allenby, hailed as a hero and at the head of representatives of the Allies, he made his formal entry into Jerusalem through the Jaffa Gate, his men marching through the stone-paved streets of the Holy City. The 10th Division was represented at the formal handover. With the fall of Jerusalem the Turks had been driven from the whole of Philistia and Judea.

The Allied line was consolidated some ten miles north of the Jerusalem-Jaffa road. The winter rains set in as the troops settled down to a period of rest and recuperation. Christmas 1917 was another bleak one for George. The third since he had left home shores. Two days before, the heavens opened and floods of rain from a torrential downpour washed the flimsy bivouacs away, even part of the vital rail line, meaning that supplies of Christmas fare, mail and even basic essentials couldn't get through. The ration was two biscuits, a tin of bully beef per gun team and a tin of jam between three gun teams. By Christmas morning George's blankets, clothes and kit were saturated.

The rain was so heavy that it was impossible for the Brigade cooks to start a fire going for a roast dinner, or the men to get together for a traditional Christmas. They had to celebrate in their cramped and dripping 'bivies' eating bully beef and wet bread, with the loss of the joyousness of the festive season. It must have seemed strange to George to spend such a miserable Christmas so near to the birthplace of Jesus. George was to find that the nights were exceptionally cold in Jerusalem due to its height above sea level.

The old British Army saying '*Roll on death, demob is too far away*' was probably on the lips of one or two soldiers at the time. To add to their troubles, the Turks decided to attack in strength just a few days after Christmas and the 10th Division were hit by the full force of the Turkish 1st Division. The Irish employed sound tactics in machine-gun and rifle fire and movement, backed up by vigorous work with the bayonet in clearing Turkish positions.

During short periods of inaction, 20th Corps arranged for parties of troops to visit the Holy City of Jerusalem and the 10th Division were pleased to take up places on the tours. While George and the likes of him felt that whilst it was wonderful to be able to visit the site of their Christian religion, to walk in the footsteps of biblical and historical figures guided by their chaplain, Jerusalem itself was an appallingly dirty, stinking dump of a place and the Holy Places, too commercialized for their liking, over-adorned as they were with cheap tawdry tinsel decorations.

It had been so even back in the eleventh century Crusades. Then, the nobles promised their Chevaliers all sorts of plunder from the Holy Land and Jerusalem in particular, but as it turned out there was very little or nothing to plunder. Certainly not enough to go round and thousands came back penniless. However, there was money to be made from the tolls charged by the erstwhile penniless Knights Templars and this became the basic economy of Jerusalem. So it was that the Knights Templars commercialized Jerusalem and the Holy Places, and this had grown to be a demeaning feature for the present day pilgrim, tourist and visitors like George and his mates.

Now moving among the Arab population, the troops found them to be dirty, smelly, and untrustworthy. The outlying villages were disgustingly filthy, with the narrow passageways between the hovels littered with refuse and communal manure heaps being kept on the roofs of the dwellings. In the aftermath of battle Arabs were seen to mutilate the wounded and rob the dead – all of which had a profound effect on the British soldier.

During this period, on 1st October, George was again promoted to substantive Lance Corporal (Paid).

The powers that be hoped that the Turkish army in Palestine could be defeated early in 1918, but a spring offensive by the Germans along the Western Front delayed General Allenby's army for nine months. The 20th Brigade returned to Egypt early in 1918 where it was based in Kantara. At this time, in a massive reorganisation, the 10th Division was 'Indianised,' with Indian units taking the place of many British. Most of the British and Irish regiments were withdrawn to France to meet the new German threat. In May, the 6th (Service) Battalion The Leinster Regiment sailed from Port Said, arriving in Marseilles on 1st June 1918 to fight on the Western Front.

George's old Brigade, the 29th, now had the following units on its strength: 1st Bn. The Leinster Regiment, 1st Bn. The Grenadier Guards, 1st Bn. 54th Sikhs, 2nd Bn. 151st Sikh Infantry and the 29th Trench Mortar Battery. His new machine gun battalion now served the three brigades in the division. It was a time of a great movement and re-deployment in the ranks of the British army in Palestine, which was to have a significant effect on George and his future conduct in the field.

His 29th Machine Gun Company was not tasked for the Western Front, leaving him and his fellow gunners in Egypt. This was a blessing in disguise as the mortality rate in the fighting in France was extremely high, and George might not have survived to the end of the war if he had been posted there.

On 7th May 1918 the 10th Battalion Machine Gun Corps was formed from the three Brigade Machine Gun Companies, (the 29th 30th and 31st); a fourth was added later making sixty-four guns in all, the new battalion supporting the 10th Division. On 19th May 1918 George was posted to the MG Battalion.

The newcomers and the 'old sweats' in the 29th Brigade and the 10th Machine Battalion spent the spring and summer of 1918 in training for future deployment. Training was carried out in some form or another during the whole of the campaign. Allenby left nothing to chance.

The survivors of that summer in the Jordan valley were now acutely gaunt and painfully thin. Most suffered from boils, malaria and septic sores and were in a poor state of health. However, the new draft of soldiers did much to bolster up the moral of the old campaigners. The training had proved to be most arduous, as the summer heat in the Jordan valley was one of endurance – it was almost unbearable between the hours of 9 a.m. and 4 p.m. Pamphlets dropped by German airmen informed the British troops that no white man could live through a summer in the valley, that even the natives retreated to the hills. The 10th Irish were to prove them wrong.

A full week's training consisted of physical training in the early morning, followed by daily inspection, handling of mules, lecture on the machine gun, lecture on working with the infantry in open warfare, gas drills, recognition and indications of targets. Laying the machine-gun for indirect fire and overhead firing (range work) covering, and advance fire, and finally bombing. This was followed by general fatigues and cleaning up the camp. At the end of a gruelling day, the men were allowed a period for games. Not much rest then!

Until 1918, the machine-gun sections had always gone forward with the attacking infantry. In the case where the infantry unit being supported by the machine-guns was beaten back, the likes of George and his fellow machine-gunners stayed out in no-man's land to give covering fire for the retreating troops. The gunners would have to wait for the night-time to make their way back to their own lines. It was this hazardous use of the gunners and their guns which led them to be named 'The Suicide Club'. From 1918 on, the guns of the machine-gun battalions were used as a covering fire, not unlike the tactic of the artillery – big guns giving covering fire from some distance behind the infantry. This system was to be used to great effect in the final stages of the Palestine Campaign.

CHAPTER 14

The finest steel has to go through the hottest fire

(Richard Nixon)

By 19th September 1918 the British were ready for a final push to defeat the Turkish Army in Palestine. Allenby's plan for the 10th Division, then holding a defensive line through the Judean Hills up to the Jordan Valley, was to mount a night attack on the Turks in a frontal assault. Then, on breaking through, to advance through the hills towards Nablus. The 1st Leinsters and the 2/151st Sikh Infantry were chosen to spearhead the main attack, supported by the rest of the 29th Brigade. The whole Division faced very stiff opposition.

Prior to that, on the 17th and 18th the Section Officers of George's 29th Company, following a recce, began laying out their line of fire and taking the necessary line of sight – then moved the guns forward into the selected gun positions. By first light the gun teams had dug and sandbagged emplacements for their weapons and prepared range charts for them. Very quietly and at night ammunition was dumped at suitable places for groups of guns deployed. Then at 19.40 on the evening of the 19th the Division began their advance, pressing forward over the very rugged country. The first objective being the Furkhah Ridge, which was six miles west of the Nablus road and ran next to the village of Lubban.

Having taken the ridge the 29th Brigade were to march to Selfit, a West Bank village two miles to the north-east and twenty miles south west of Nablus. The line of attack was from the west up to the spurs from the Wadi Rashid.

The ridge was the whole pivot of the enemy's defensive line on this part of the front. It was more strongly fortified than any position opposite 20th Corps. Here again the Turks had employed all their ingenuity in constructing works a mile and a half to the north-west, to resist an attack from the south. It was to be a fatal mistake.

Since the line opposite Furkhah had been held, the 20th Corps set out to lead the enemy to anticipate that they would assault the position from the south. Nothing was ever attempted against the western spurs of the ridge and the result was that the Turks left the ground rising up to Furkhah from both sides of the Wadi Rashid in a comparatively weak state of defence. Yet the policy of the 20th Corps was always to attack up these spurs. When it came, the attack on Furkhah was a double disappointment to the enemy. It came from a direction the Turks hadn't provided for and it fell on them at their most vulnerable moment.

The enemy troops on the front of the attack had received orders to retire at eight o'clock. The 29th Brigade's attack was timed a quarter of an hour earlier. Instead of the enemy surprising their attackers by leaving empty trenches, the opening bombardment and a machine-gun barrage in which George was involved, was deadly in its effect. During the action that followed, the four machine gun companies (32 guns per company) expended (fired) 125,000 rounds (bullets).

George's war with 'Johnny Turk'[3] was very personal. At times it became a battle of machine-guns, machine-gun against machine-gun with their never-ending pit-pit-pit sounds, the outcome dependent on the coolness of each individual Gunner.

In many cases the machine gunners and their guns were lifesavers, with their very presence inspiring the infantry with confidence.

[3] Nicknames for the Turks; Abdul – Jacko – Johnny Turk – Johnny T and Mr. J.T.

However, George and his fellow gunners were the object of very special attention from the Turkish artillery and snipers, whose discovery and recording of their positions was a matter of the keenest observation. George had seen the effects of accurate sniper fire on fellow gunners where, in a close-range head shot, the skull opens up like a flower. The Snipers were known to the men as 'Body Snatchers.' Despite that, George and the machine gunners of the 29th Company came into their own as they pinned down the enemy, paving the way for the 29th Brigade infantry to attack.

The Irish were stoutly opposed at first, but nothing could stop them. They came under very heavy enemy fire as they captured the enemy strongholds with the bayonet. The sudden appearance in the enemy trench lines caused great confusion to the hapless Turks. They raked the dug-outs behind the fire trenches with the bayonet. In the desperate circumstances, the Irish went about it with great ferocity as they passed along the trench line, sticking and dropping the enemy, trampling them underfoot in a frightful scramble of blood-lust and sicking death. Enemy soldiers dropped their arms and threw up their hands. The speed with which the Irish gained the trenches made the Turks realise that they were irresistible and soon all opposition broke down. Here was the element of surprise with a vengeance.

> 'One sergeant, whose entire gun team had become casualties, sat at his gun alone surrounded by the corpses of his comrades. His ammunition was getting low, he could not leave his gun, and had no one to send for a fresh supply. Just, as his last belt was running through the feed block, a giant Turk appeared over the crest of the hill, his bayonet held out before him, his eyes staring as though mesmerized… but the sergeant, who had kept a few cartridges for the end, with some rapid turns of the wheel,

elevated his gun, aimed point-blank at his adversary, and pressed the thumb piece... the Turk suddenly crumpled up, his arms shot forward over the gun, and his rifle fell with a clatter on the stones.

The centre of the cone of fire had caught him in the throat, severing his head from his body; the blood from the headless trunk poured in a red stream over the sergeant's khaki tunic as he sat at his gun transfixed.'

(Vivian Gilbert, Machine Gun Company commander (*Hell in the Holy land*), David R. Woodward.)

Surprised and unprepared the Turkish/German army fell into a disorganised retreat in which the Turkish H.Q. Garrison at Nazareth was captured. The Division gave the enemy no respite as they pressed forward to block the Turk's escape route from Nablus, along the Wadi Farah to the Jordan River. Although the men and animals were dead tired, driven on to exhaustion they were ordered to pursue the enemy relentlessly if there were any signs of a general retreat. The battalions forged ahead from the ridge with the machine gun section 'leap-frogging' in support. As they advanced towards their objective, they encountered heavy machine-gun and rifle fire. The Infantry and the gunners met Johnny Turk in the open and gave him all the lead he asked for. The Turk was not keen on a fire-fight in the open and even less keen about the advance of the Irish with fixed bayonets.

George's 'D' section (3 to 4 guns) slowly worked forward in support of Battalions of the 29th Brigade and in the early morning of the 29th his Section materially assisted the infantry in the capture and consolidation of hill 2264 (Selfit). He had to operate his weapon with enemy bullets whizzing around him, deafened by the constant roar of artillery causing an everlasting din.

The rounds spewing from his gun sounded like an iron rod being run over a corrugated metal sheet. The empty cases, ejecting from the weapons' extractor, built a glittering pile around George and his weapon. Finally, under the onslaught the attackers broke the opposition, with the Turks falling back to the village of Selfit. It was during the entire phase of attack that George Joseph Adamson was to distinguish himself and for his gallantry was awarded the DCM. The citation for the award of the Distinguished Conduct Medal[4] in the *London Gazette* for 17th April 1919 reads:

'48507 Pte. (A/ L/ Cpl.) G. Adamson, 10th M.G. Bn. M.G. Co of (Moate, Co. Westmeath) (EGYPT):

'For conspicuous gallantry on the 20th September 1918 near Selfit. When the enemy made an attempt to capture his gun, this N.C.O. continued to fire with the greatest coolness and disregard for danger although he was being very heavily engaged with enemy shell and machine-gun fire. Throughout the day, he behaved with extreme gallantry.'

(All this from a soldier who, from the period 18th April 1918 to 1st October had been promoted to NCO rank, busted to Private and re-promoted three times. George seems to have questioned authority from time to time to say the least, but there is no doubting his qualities as a fighting soldier.)

Following on from this action, his 'D' Section then secured excellent targets in the shape of enemy troops and transport, moving along the Iskaka-Yasuf Road. They also engaged an enemy artillery battery whose fire, in addition to that of hostile machine guns, was considerably reduced. After the battle the Infantry spoke highly of the work of George's section, both in covering their advance on Hill 2264 and later helping them to hold it.

At 04.00 on the morning of the 10th, George's Section moved

---

[4] The Distinguished Conduct Medal was instituted on December 4th 1854 during the Crimean War as a reward for bravery in action by 'other ranks' non-commissioned officers and men of the British and Empire armies. The medal was 'usually accompanied by a gratuity of 20 pounds and a small pension.'

up the Wadi Mutwy to take up positions on the high ground in Biddich, to cover the line of advance of the infantry on the line Haris-Ras Aish where they were able to cover the advance to the objective. At this stage of the battle, if you could have asked George what he was fighting for, he may well have replied, *for those who clung to the ground next to him.*

At 23.00 hours on the 20th, the 29th Company resumed its advance with the 29th Brigade along the Selfit-Iskaka Road and arrived at Kuzah. At midday on 21st the Company proceeded along the Nablus Road to Balata near Nablus, where two sections finally engaged the enemy as they retreated in disorder, the company capturing many prisoners. At four o'clock on the morning of 21st September, the 10th Division having gained all objectives and more, held firm defensive positions. They were entrenched along a line from Selfit, about 20 kilometres south west of Nablus and the small village of Senameh, having advanced a mile and a half from their start point and cutting the Turkish supply line on the Nablus-Jerusalem road. Fighting eventually began to slow during the late afternoon, until it eventually ceased at dusk. On that memorable evening, the men were past exhaustion. They had fought all through the night and the next day. They had charged and stormed the enemy trenches and defence lines almost non-stop, so it was not surprising to find men dropping down with sheer weariness, added to which was the problem of water. Eventually the order went round that they could rest a while, and the men sank down in the captured trenches that stank of blood and the unhygienic habits of Johnny Turk, sleeping the sleep of exhaustion.

During the series of attacks in their advance to contact, George's and the rest of the machine-gun teams would have had to physically man-handle their guns, ammo and equipment from one position to another, as there would have been no time to load up the battalion mules. The word 'exhaustion' is not strong enough to convey the state of the gunners when the cease-fire was given. The 29th Company later moved to bivouac at Azmut.

The pre-battle training had finally paid off. The 10th Division eventually captured Nablus, where during the action they took 1,223 prisoners. General Longley, General Officer Commanding could be immensely proud of his Division's splendid performance throughout the night attack, which entailed heavy marches over very rough ground, pushing through rock strewn ravines and up rugged peaks against stiff opposition from a determined enemy. The Turks fought bravely with screams of '*Allah, Allah*'.

The Battle of Megiddo, which followed, brought about the destruction of the Turkish army in Palestine. On 9th March the 10th Division advanced northwards at great speed, with an attack on Wadi el JibIt. The attack was a great success and was followed up the next day by further advances and successful actions until 12th March, when all objectives had been achieved. This was followed in April by a successful assault on the high peak called 'Grey Rock.'

The Division, back on the attack again, continued a left wheeling movement into the hills and started to roll up the Turkish flank, beating down all enemy opposition. Then on 20th September after a forced march of some twenty-four miles over broken and rough country, the Division occupied Shechem, the chief city of Samaria.

The main attack on 18th September was so successful, all infantry actions finished on the 20th. With that, the war in Palestine ended for them. It was Allenby's final triumph in which the 10th Division and Irishmen like George played no small part.

During negotiations on the island of Mudros in the Aegean, the Turkish government was compelled to sign an armistice on 28th

October 1918, ending all hostilities and bringing an end to centuries of rule by the Ottoman Empire in the Middle East. Prior to that, the Allied army in Salonika had defeated the Bulgarians and their allies. Then on the 11th November 1918 the armistice came into effect, bringing an end to the carnage and slaughter. So, the *'war to end all wars'* came to an end.

12th November the 10th (Irish) Division concentrated at Sarafand, ready for a move to Egypt. By 1st December it was back again in Cairo. Sad to say, when an epidemic of influenza and malaria broke out all the 'old sweats' whose blood had thinned over four and half years of war were the first to fall to the ravages of illness, and many who had survived the war years were to die with the end of their enlistment and homecoming in sight.

On 4th January 1919, George was promoted to Acting Corporal and to Acting Sergeant on the 6th, a temporary rank which he held to 28th January 1919, reverting to Acting Corporal on 29th January 1919. In that rank on 12th February 1919 he embarked at Port Said on a troop ship bound for England.

George had been upwards of four years on active service, during which his life and the lives of all the Irishmen in the 10th Division had resembled the Roman legions, who were often left for long periods on the outskirts of the empire. He had seen diverse fighting and tackled the Bulgar in Macedonia and the Turk in Palestine. All the time, with the exception of a few days at Salonika, Egypt and Palestine, he and his fellow Irishmen had been remote from civilization. He had hardly seen a town, just the dirty hamlets of the Struma valley and the wretched villages of the Palestine uplands.

He had lived in the open in the most astonishing varieties of weather, from the tropical heat where flies disputed his food and mosquitoes heralded fever, to times when the snow lay ten feet deep in the sunken hill tracks. Leave had generally meant the dubious attractions of Salonika or the inevitable disillusionment of Jerusalem.

George and his mates had been wanderers and they would bring home many strange impressions to ponder on. This at least they surely brought back – the knowledge they had served their country (Ireland) well and carried out boldly every task put to them. From 1914 to 1918 the 10th (Irish) Division suffered a loss of 9,363, all ranks killed, missing or wounded in action.

'I, too, have been a victim,
aggressor sometimes too,
but don't dare tell me what pain is
when you've no inkling what I've been through.'

(Unknown)

John Redmond MP who encouraged many young Irishmen to join the British army, including his own brother, did not live to see the end of the war as he died on 6th March 1918 in London, aged 62. He didn't live to witness the failure of his Home Rule Plan. On 19th November 1915 he had visited the Irish troops in France. His speech to the men of The Royal Irish Rifles is summarized by Chaplain Father Gill:

> *'He was glad to meet a regiment which contained men of every creed from so many different parts of Ireland, especially the North. They were now brothers-in-arms, and he was sure their harmony and unity in the great cause in which they were fighting was a happy omen of relations which would exist between all in Ireland after the war.'*

Unfortunately, his prophecy was falsified by future events. His remains were removed to Wexford in Ireland, his internment taking place in an ancient cemetery near his ancestral home at Aughvana.

Major William (Willie) Redmond, brother of John Redmond, was killed on the first day of the Battle of Messines in 1917 while serving with the 16th Division. Upset by the execution of the leaders of the Easter Revolution, he left instructions that should he die in the war, he was not to be buried in a British Military cemetery. Instead he was buried outside the walls of the military cemetery at Loker.

Of the estimated 120,000 to 210,000 Irishmen who fought in World War One, about 53,000 were Protestant and 65,000 Catholic; around 30,000 to 60,000 paid the ultimate price. Twenty-three Irishmen were awarded the Victoria Cross.

'The virtual disappearance of the World War from the version of Irish history taught to the first two generations of the new independent Irish State had the result that few were aware of the extent of the Irish participation in the actual fighting.'
(Department of the Taoiseach – *Irish Soldiers of the First World War*.)

'If any question why we died tell them, because our fathers lied.'
(Rudyard Kipling)

CHAPTER 15

DEMOBILIZATION

*It hurts to find out what you wanted doesn't match
what you dreamed about it would be.*

(Randy K. Milholland).

On arrival in UK George was transported from the dock to London, where he travelled by train to No.1 Dispersal Unit at Oswestry in Shropshire, England. There on 1st March 1919, having served for four years and thirty-eight days with the colours, he was discharged from the British Army. Apart from his award of the DCM, George received three campaign medals. The 1914-15 Star, The British War Medal and the Victory Medal. His demob certificate states that:

> *'The above-named soldier is granted a 28 days furlough from the date stamped herein pending.'*

George had to sign to the effect that: *'I have received an advance of 2 pounds.'*

Added to this, he was given a clothing allowance, a rail warrant and up to 29 weeks unemployment benefits with a war gratuity based on rank and service. Further to this he received 14 shillings per week for his award of the DCM, plus a gratuity of twenty pounds. A certificate from the Royal Hospital in Chelsea in London awarded him 6 pence per day disablement pension. It is believed that this could have been for dysentery, or malaria contracted in Salonika or Palestine.

His wartime experience, where he had looked at death in the eye and survived not once, but many times, saw him grow from a young lad into a man, reaching a high degree of maturity as a non-commissioned officer in charge of a gun and gun crew. A hero to the British, who had awarded him a high honour. Forged in the heat of battle he had become cool, confident and astute. He would take no crap from anyone. The service had also given him self-discipline, leadership skills, a ruthless streak and a healthy sense of who he was, all of which would stand him in good stead in the years to come.

Finally, on 31st March 1919 George's war ended. Now it was time to go home and he was looking forward to being in the bosom of his family again, to live in the peace and freedom of an independent Ireland which he had fought and suffered for like so many of his comrades – whereas thousands of his fellow Irishmen would never see Ireland again. Those young Irishmen in their teens and twenties knew they were about to die, yet in their letters they demonstrated their belief that their deaths would contribute to a better world and the freedom of their homeland. However, sad to say, Ireland was never to get Home Rule.

For the surviving Irish Volunteers returning from the war, many of whom were suffering and would continue to suffer from traumatic stress disorder or shell-shock as it was then known, for the rest of their lives, were treated with hostility by the people of Ireland. They were tended to be seen as spies, or agents for the British Forces. It was not be until 1966 that they were acknowledged for their sacrifices by the Irish Government and the Irish people. On his return to Ireland after demobilization, George was lucky enough to get employment in the Pump House with the Great Southern and Western Railway Station (now Athlone Station), Athlone. He worked there for about three months with his friend Christopher 'Kit' McKeown from his hometown of Moate. It was while they were working together that they re-joined the Irish Volunteers. George's goal of Irish Freedom, having remained unfulfilled, did not affect him in a depressive way. It only strengthened his resolve.

Having failed to gain freedom and peace for his native land by joining the British Army and fighting in the Great War, he had decided to try again. In becoming a revolutionary soldier he forfeited his British Army pensions, including payments for his Distinguished Conduct Medal. In his new calling he teamed up with his schoolboy companion and friend Jim Tormey, then a Commandant and Quartermaster for the Athlone Brigade, Irish Volunteers.

James (Jim) Tormey was described by Volunteer David Daly in 1920 as being a man of splendid physique, good appearance and military bearing. Like George, he was born in Moate, Co. Westmeath in 1895. Enlisted in the British Army in Galway on 18th February 1915, Army Number 3876, he served one year and twenty-eight days with the 5th Battalion Connaught Rangers.

On 5th August 1915, as a Lance Corporal, he landed at Anzac Cove on the Gallipoli peninsula in the Dardenelles, taking part in the bitter fighting and seeing action on San Bair, Hill 60, Kabak Kuyu wells and Chunuk Bay. Due to illness or injury he was posted to the 3rd (Reserve) Battalion stationed in Galway where he had enlisted. Six months later (on 15th March 1916) he was discharged as being medically unfit for further war service. Awarded the 1914-1918 Star, The British War Medal and the Victory Medal, he would be seen to be a skilled and gallant soldier by his future actions.

The following narrative, quotations and dialogue outline the deeds and the hell the Athlone Brigade raised in and around their operational area and the enemies they faced, in particular the notorious Black and Tans.

CHAPTER 16

THE IRISH WAR OF INDEPENDENCE
21st January 1919 – 11th July 1921

*'Life springs from death; and from the graves of patriot men and
women spring living nations. The defenders of this realm…think
they have pacified Ireland…but the fools, the fools, the fools! They
have left us our Fenian dead, and while Ireland holds these graves,
Ireland unfree shall never be at peace.'*

(The burial of O'Donavan Rossa in Glasnevin Cemetery.
Padraic Pearse's famous oration.)

The Irish Volunteers was formed on 25th March 1913 by Eoin
McNeill and The O'Rahilly (A section of which broke away when
John Redmond advocated fighting for England in September 1914
and became known as The National Volunteers).

The 1914 Constitution of the Irish Volunteers:

*'To train, discipline and equip for the purpose (To secure and
maintain the rights and liberties common to all the people of
Ireland) an Irish Volunteer Force which will render service to
an Irish National Government when such is established.'*

The Midland Volunteer Force was set up in Athlone as a
battalion in 1913, which by 1919 had become the Irish Volunteers.
When the Athlone Brigade was formed, it had as O/C's (Officers

Commanding) Tom 'Con' Costello, Sean Hurley and Seamus O'Meara. George, because of his military training and his wartime experience, soon gained promotion to become a Vice O/C of the Brigade. Such ex-servicemen as George and Jim Tormey brought to the Volunteers a knowledge of soldiering and arms, and were ingrained with a ruthlessness in combat. They set about applying their military skills. Each company was expected to parade one night per week, parades and meetings to be held in secret.

During parade nights, George and Jim trained the men in foot drill, marching and instruction in weapon handling, fire and movement, ambush drills, scouting, battlefield first aid and methods of instruction. This was carried out in O'Connells Field and Mount Hussey, and in units all over the Brigade area. In the case of the Coosan and Summerhill units, what few weapons that were available at the time were shared for drilling and instructions in their use. They were often borrowed from the other Volunteers, otherwise the boys had to raid for them. They were supplemented by hurling sticks and roughly fashioned wooden rifles.

There were very important week-long training camps on the out-farm of James Lynch, Annsfield, Baylough, next to Halls Bridge in Athlone, at Crannagh in south Roscommon, which was given over to the Volunteers as a training base, and another training camp at Benown, both set in desolate areas of the countryside in the great outdoors. There were also training camps at Drumraney and on islands in Lough Ree, most notably the Hare and Friars Islands. In these camps, the Volunteers were mainly taught field craft, how to set up and rehearse tactical exercises, manoeuvres and schemes. George taught them how to see the terrain, not the scenery, and how to use it.

Dinner Parade, Coosan Camp, Sandy Bay, Coosan, Co. Westmeath
(Photograph Courtesy of Cork Museum)

Generally, route marches and other exercises were conducted at weekends. Specialised training took the form of railway demolition and general demolitions, road mining, tree felling for road blocks and the use of automatic weapons and machine guns. George and Jim also ran separate classes for officers and section leaders. The Brigade strength was numbered at about a thousand and comprised of local companies and battalions, each depending on the strength of the local population. In general companies were small in strength, roughly about a platoon; twenty to thirty men in all, while others as high as forty to fifty Volunteers. Each unit had a large number of part-time Volunteers who would assemble when needed for a particular operation and provide intelligence and a whole range of other services.

The intelligence organisations within the companies and battalions was generally used to keep watch on the movements of people not in sympathy with the Volunteers, or suspected of conveying information to the enemy. Every Volunteer was an intelligence agent, his duty to report any incident that came to his notice and in particular, to keep a check on enemy movements and tabulate the regularity of their patrols and so forth. Intelligence in the area was maintained by a Volunteer called O'Brien who worked in the Athlone Post Office and who rendered valuable service.

The system was extremely flexible, to minimize damage, and it worked perfectly. The Brigade area covered South Roscommon and Westmeath, from Knockcrogny to the Shannon River and southwards to Athlone. It included the Athlone, Bealnamulla, Drumraney, Moate and Summerhill areas, with Volunteers from South Roscommon and South Westmeath operating in the Athlone Brigade area, which was made up of the following units: 1st Battalion, Athlone Area, 2nd Battalion, Drumraney Area, 3rd Battalion, Summerhill. A battalion consisted of about four hundred men and was commanded by a Commandant, divided into four companies, each commanded by a Captain.

The companies at Clonown, Curraghboy, Drum Moore and Taughmaconnel were also part of the Athlone Battalion. Communications were maintained throughout the area by means of dispatch riders on cycles, motorcycle and even horseback. Some Brigade officers had to make long and hazardous journeys to attend Brigade Council meetings.

Each Volunteer was expected to have the following equipment ready for mobilisation: A small pack or haversack, water bottle, spare pair of boots, socks, towel and soap, twenty four-hours rations, bundle of kindling wood and mess tins or tin plates and mug. The Volunteers also paid a small subscription, from sixpence a week to a shilling per month for the purchase of arms and other expenses including on-going actions against enemy forces, including ambushes, destroying R.I.C. Barracks, maintaining arms dumps and hideouts, scouting and collecting intelligence.

It was not easy to join the Volunteers as, apart from being a hush-hush organisation, it was selective regarding the type of men allowed into the ranks. Only men of good standing, from decent families who were deemed to be reliable in every way and endowed with a strong national outlook were accepted for the force. The reason behind this was that the country had such a long history of failures through the activities of informers. It was only natural that the Volunteers should be very careful.

CHAPTER 17

Some people make headlines while others make history.

(Philip Elmer-de-Witt)

On 14th December 1918 a general election was held and the Sinn Fein organisation, the political side of the independence movement, contested all seats in the country, the vast majority being held by the Irish Parliamentary Party led by John Dillon following the death of John Redmond. Sinn Fein candidates, if elected, pledged not to take their seats in the British parliament and, in effect, to boycott the body and establish an Irish Government in Dublin. This complete departure in Irish Politics appealed to the Irish people, in view of the frustrated efforts of the IPP to secure some measure of self-government from Britain. The greatest amount of the work towards a successful election result for Sinn Fein was performed by the Volunteers. The landslide victory that followed was a resounding one for Sinn Fein and a catastrophic defeat for the Parliamentary Party, which was practically wiped out.

> *'In the two years after the Easter Rebellion, nationalists began to support the Sinn Fein Party which supported complete independence from Britain instead of the Home Rule Party of John Redmond. In the General Election of 1918 the once powerful Home Rule Party was swept aside and the Sinn Fein*

candidates won overwhelming victory. In the election the Home Rule Party was reduced to a mere six seats under the new leadership of John Dillon.'

(Mike Ryan: Mount Temple School, Dublin).

The newly elected Sinn Fein members of Parliament refused to take their seats in Westminster on the opening of Parliament. Instead, on 21st January 1919, and despite the fact that quite a few of Sinn Fein MPs were still in jail during this period, the remainder met in the Round Room of the Mansion House in Dublin. There they declared their allegiance to the Proclamation of 1916, read out by Patrick Pearse outside the GPO Easter 1916, setting up a revolutionary parliament called Dail Eireann / Assembly of Ireland on a democratic basis, in what was to be the first Irish Government since the Act of Union.

The new Dail appointed ministers to different departments of state and took over responsibility for the Volunteer organisation when they instituted the Army of the Republic, with Richard Mulcathy as its first minister. From August onwards the Volunteers became known as The Irish Republican Army or IRA.

Initially, no oath was taken by Volunteers on enlistment since 1917; however the Dail now declared that every Volunteer and officer would have to take an Oath of Allegiance to the Irish Republic as follows:

'I, .., do solemnly swear (or affirm) that I do not and shall not yield a voluntary support to any pretended Government, authority or power within Ireland hostile and inimical thereto, and I do further swear (or affirm) that to the best of my knowledge and ability I will support and defend the Irish Republic and the Government of the Irish Republic, which is

Dail Eireann, against all enemies, foreign or domestic, and I will bear true faith and allegiance to the same, and I take this obligation freely without any mental reservation or purpose of evasion, so help me, God.'

No persuasion or force was to be used to induce Volunteers to take this Oath as everyone was quite free not to do so if they liked. Anyone declining to take the Oath would cease to be a Volunteer. Our officers and men took the Oath without hesitation and as far as I can remember, there were no defaulters.

(Thomas Kieran, Moate Company, Irish Volunteers – *Witness Statement No: 1594 to the Bureau of Military History.*)

On the same day as the Mansion House meeting and the declaration of the Irish Republic, an action by the Volunteers, believed to have started the Anglo-Irish War, was typical of the type of actions that followed.

It occurred on Tuesday 21st January 1919 between 12.30 and 1 p.m. at Soloheadbeg, a small townland some two miles outside Tipperary Town near Limerick Junction railway station. Two RIC officers named as Constables James McDonnell aged 50 from Belmullet, a widower with four children and Patrick O'Connell, aged about 30, a single man from Coachford Co. Cork, both Irish born Catholics and popular in the community they served, were escorting on foot a horse-drawn cart, carrying a quantity of gelignite from Tipperary Military Barracks.

Volunteers Dan Breen, Tadhg Crowe, Sean Hogan, Paddy McCormack, Paddy O'Dwyer, Sean O'Meara, Micheal Ryan, Seamus Robinson and Sean Tracey (Ryan and O'Meara were both cycle scouts), had planned the ambush of the four-man party, disarm the RIC escort and then make off with the arms and explosives. Dail Eireann and Sinn Fein had not been informed or consulted about the attack beforehand.

The officers were both armed with rifles which were loaded and ready to defend their charge. As the ambush was sprung the Volunteers, wearing masks, jumped over the roadside fence and shouted, '*Hands up!*' The constables brought their weapons into the aim and were met with accurate fire from Volunteers which killed them. The driver of the cart, James Godfrey, and Patrick Flynn, another County Council employee, were both unharmed. After loading up the constables' rifles and ammunition, Hogan drove the cart away with Tracy and Breen in the direction of the quarry. Witnesses stated it was driven towards Dundrum, Co. Tipperary.

When the horse and cart was later found abandoned at Allen Creamery near Dundrum, it was minus the gelignite. This type of action is how the Volunteers obtained arms, ammunition and explosives, as well as hitting back at the forces of the Crown.

The incident was quickly followed by the Imposition of Martial Law in the area and wanted posters offering a ten thousand pounds reward for information leading to the arrest of Dan Breen were posted on the notice boards of every RIC barracks.

Breen later recalled:

> '...we took the action deliberately, having thought over the matter and talked between us. Treacy had stated to me that the only way of starting a war was to kill someone, and we wanted to start a war, so we intended to kill some of the police whom we looked upon as the foremost and most important branch of the enemy forces. The only regret that we had following the ambush was that there were only two policemen in it, instead of the six we expected.'

The Constabulary (Ireland) Act established the first national police force in Ireland, incorporating the county constabularies that had been in existence since 1822. It was renamed the Royal Irish Constabulary for its work in helping to suppress the Fenian uprising of 1867. They, the native police force of Ireland, the law of the land, were made up of almost 70% Irishmen. Rigorous checks were made on new recruits to the RIC by their local barracks. The results were sent to their HQ in Dublin Castle, from where they were centrally controlled for further investigation, to ascertain if the prospective candidate had any connections whatsoever with Republicanism.

Successful applicants were sent to the RIC Training Depot in Phoenix Park, Dublin for six-months basic training, where they dressed in dark-green uniforms and were subject to military-style discipline and drill, at the end of which they were posted to one of the 1,600 RIC barracks dotted throughout the country. Officers could not serve in their own native counties and they had to serve at least seven years before being allowed to marry. Having been vetted by a superior, the married couple were transferred to a county where they had no relatives. The constables were the eyes and ears of the British administration in Dublin Castle and engaged in surveillance of known or suspected subversives. They also had considerable civil and local government responsibility. A constable's main duty was to write weekly reports on new faces and any suspicious happenings on his patch, with the emphasis on anti-British actions and utterings; the actual investigation of local crime was not a priority. They supervised and paid informers and spies, while they themselves were *ipso factor* informers and spies and were the front line in the fight against the Freedom Fighters. The RIC did not answer to the local authorities and could only be dismissed from service on orders from Dublin Castle.

The force operated from barracks situated every few miles

around the countryside, their posts in 1919 were a mass of barbed wire, sandbags and steel shutters. They became a target for every IRA unit in the country.

The awful part of the RIC was that they were Irishmen of the same stock as the Volunteers and their fellow countrymen. There was always a void between the people and the RIC since the Rebellion in 1916. But there were one or two policemen who favoured and helped the Republican cause as much as possible.

CHAPTER 18

Without the help of the people our exertions would be as nothing

(Charles Stuart Parnell)

The delegation that the Irish Volunteer's Executive sent to the 1919 Paris Peace Conference did not succeed in gaining international support. It appeared to the movement that as political means had failed, the only way now was to pursue independence through military action. Seamus O'Meara from Bay Lough, Athlone, who was a butcher with premises in Connaught Street, Athlone, and was then O/C of the Athlone Brigade, was called to a meeting at GHQ in Dublin at the end of 1919. There, he was told that the Executive had endorsed violent attacks upon Crown forces and that it was time the Volunteers became more active.

Meanwhile the activity of the Volunteers was dispersed, erratic and small-scale. They were vastly outnumbered and pitched battles were suicidal. Small ambushes and raids were as close as they could get to hounding the British forces, so they employed the tactic of 'shoot and scoot'.

This, the start of the War for Independence, was considered by the British authorities as merely a nuisance phase which would eventually stop. Its full implication had not, as yet, been fully realized by the government or the general public.

Attacks mainly concerned the acquisition of arms, the

disruption of services and motored traffic on major and minor roads by cutting deep trenches, felling trees and the destruction of evacuated RIC barracks in the county. Volunteers in Kilbeggan on New Year's Day raided six homes, (one raid actually on New Year's Eve) searching for arms. They managed to gain five shotguns and a number of sporting cartridges. In one of the raids, they failed to procure any so they fired some shots and left. During this time raids by the Ballykeeran Company brought in approximately forty shotguns.

Then the volunteers had a stroke of luck when a plane carrying ammunition made a forced landing at Keelogues, where a group of Volunteers from the 3rd Battalion, Athlone Brigade seized its contents. However, the Tans also got lucky when they raided the home of John Harney of Crannagh, Drum, a Volunteer with the Battalion, where they found rifles and guns in his hayloft, for which he was sent to Mountjoy Prison.

Shortage of weapons was the main complaint of most companies. It would appear that Athlone and Kilbeggan were the most active areas where raiding for arms occurred, illustrating that the most active companies were willing to procure their own arms. Weapons were never stored in buildings in case of a raid by the military, but stored in wooden boxes and buried in walls or in a sandpit, being the driest places around and in faces of turf banks. Unfortunately the ammunition deteriorated owing to damp despite all efforts to protect it. It was hard to store cartridges under those conditions as the compressed paper from which the casing was made absorbed the damp or moisture from the air and became swollen. This made them difficult to load into the guns and hard to extract, as they dried out and expanded in the barrels when fired.

In some units where no guns were available, the men were issued with pikes made from parts of scrap cars and vans in Moyvore by

Joe Burke the blacksmith and by Willie John Byrne in his forge in Athlone. Ash poles were made to fit the pikes and stored in a separate location to the pike heads. The pikes were carried in a parade to the hill of Uisneach, to a meeting organised by Countess Plunkett demanding the release of prisoners in 1919. Willie John also made a mould for the production of buckshot, which was loaded into shotgun cartridges after the ordinary shot was removed and homemade bombs of the canister type which were filled with gelignite and fitted with a detonator.

The construction of the bombs used in the war was not an exact science. The producer had to guess the amount of explosives to be used and had to improvise a container. There was a general formula but frequently the bomb maker had to be approximate, or sometimes substitute. Cement mines were formed in one and a half feet square cases of wood; the cement then mixed with sand but with the centre left empty to take the varying amounts of gelignite, then capped over with pitch, the fuse going down the middle of the frame. An electric detonator would ignite it, thus giving the bomber a choice of using batteries or a fuse.

At the back of the Kenny house which was raided many times, was a small dwelling in the bog used as a meeting point and a place to sleep for the Volunteers. When they assembled, they never carried their weapons for fear of a raid when they would be confiscated, so they were stacked some hundred yards or more away from the house. Volunteers also had guns hidden in a cave in Ardkeenan which they retained during the 'Troubles.'

The Volunteers benefited from the widespread help given to them by the general Irish population, who refused to pass on information to the RIC and the British military and often provided 'safe houses' and provisions to men 'on the run'. The Volunteers had the utmost admiration and praise for the local people throughout the Brigade area, who made their homes, food and a change of clothes available to them. They took the risk of being shot, or having their homes and property burnt to the ground and imprisonment for the whole family if they were found to be harbouring wanted men. The Brigade had a network of houses throughout its area of operations. Without such aid, they couldn't have operated.

No doubt that much of the IRA's popularity arose from the excessive reaction of the British forces to the activity of the Volunteers. But, perhaps the greatest admiration was reserved for their female comrades in the *Cumann na mBan:* (Women's League), Auxiliary force of Irish Volunteers.

Annie O'Connor from Church Street Athlone, a typical example of the brave women of the *Cumann*, participated in the Parliamentary election, drilled and took classes in first aid, collected money and helped to organise dances to raise more money for the cause; from October 1919, she became involved in the military work of the Volunteers, carrying dispatches and doing intelligence work; then, acting as an armed scout for an attempted ambush at Clonown and taking two wounded volunteers into her home and organised medical treatment for them. She became a special courier for the Athlone Brigade, carrying ammunition, batteries, bomb detonators and electrical cables from Dublin to Athlone by train, and bought ammunition and a rifle from a British soldier in Athlone and carried them through the town in broad daylight.

However, this type of cooperation by the general public was not evident in Athlone, which had a large presence of British Military. The town, in particular Irishtown, was particularly ill disposed. It was an unfriendly territory with the local people hostile to the Volunteers, mainly because there was a preponderance of war wives and families of men serving in the British Army drawing separation monies from the British Government.

'Their only fear was that the war would come to a sudden end.'

It was not an easy decision to become an active Volunteer. For example, back on 3rd November 1919, the Bishop of Meath had called down the curse of God on the Volunteer who shot an RIC Constable in Bellivor (Co. Meath). In such a strictly religious society, evidence like this illustrates that volunteer activists were much marginalized from the general public.

The fact that there was no support from the Irish Catholic hierarchy and, to a lesser extent the press, was a constant source of pain and heart-searching for the Volunteers.

In order to step up attacks on the forces of the Crown, Seamus O'Meara was ordered by GHQ Dublin to lead raids on police barracks from February 1920. In the same month County Westmeath was proclaimed as being in a state of disturbance.

CHAPTER 19

THE BLACK AND TANS

The most select crowd of blackguards ever inflicted on our country.
(Mossie Harnett & James Joy, 'Victory or Woe')

The British Government's response to the increase in violence was to recruit an irregular force of paramilitary police, drafted into Ireland on 25th March 1920 to beef up the Royal Irish Constabulary, depleted by desertions, killings and resignations. This new force was nicknamed the 'Black and Tans' (in Irish, na Duchronaigh) due to their distinctive and haphazard dress of mixed military and police uniforms, with dark- green caps, black tunics and khaki trousers. In Limerick, their uniform code was compared to a famous pack of foxhounds, the Scateen Black and Tans whose colours and demeanour were similar. The Tans were an undisciplined quasi-military and, in essence, a mercenary force. Given six weeks training in the Curragh Camp, Co. Kildare and armed with Colt .45 Automatic pistols and Martini-Metford carbines, they were rapidly posted to RIC barracks throughout Ireland. Their pay, ten shillings a day plus full board and lodgings, a goodly sum for the period when compared to the one shilling per day paid to soldiers in the British Army.

The force composed of mainly British (English), Scots, or Welsh, most were ex-soldiers traumatized from trench warfare in The Great War, with a sprinkling of Northern Irish Orangemen, ex-convicts and thugs. Their main role, to strengthen the military might of police posts where they functioned as sentries, guards, escorts for government agents, reinforcement for the RIC and mounting a determined counter-insurgency campaign.

The object, apparently of the Government in letting loose this force in the country, was to create a reign of terror and break the Irish resistance movement. The *raison d'être* of the Tans: the elimination of the Nationalist threat and to make Ireland *'hell for the rebels to live in'*. In doing so, they employed brutal, indiscriminate and sadistic force on guilty and innocent alike. As the Lord Lieutenant Sir John French said, *'The Irish should be crushed as one would crush a poisonous insect.'*

They were not subject to strict military discipline in their early months in Ireland, and as a result, the deaths of Black and Tans at the hands of the IRA were often repaid with arbitrary reprisals against the civilian population. They quickly gained a reputation for drunkenness and ill discipline, becoming notorious through their numerous attacks on civilians. Stranded in a hostile countryside, they relieved their boredom by helping themselves to the wares of local shops, raiding and sometimes demolishing homes and bludgeoning Volunteers.

The 8,000 strong Tan force was supplemented by an additional unit of 1,500 ex-army officers, The Auxiliary Division, nicknamed the Auxies, or Cadets. Their rank was equivalent in status of a Detective Sergeant in the RIC. Mostly ex-British Army officers, they elected their own commanders.

They wore Glengarry bonnets with mixed military uniforms, armed with Webley .45 pistols. Their pay, one pound per day, double the wages of the Black and Tans. They were formed into companies of 70 / 80 up to 100 men and stationed in an area of unrest. The mission of both groups was to terrorise.

'Their reputation was just as bad as the Tans, for their mistreatment of the civilian population and they were

considered to be more ruthless and more intelligent than the Tans and tended to be more effective and more willing to take on the IRA. These two groups became known as "Tudor's Toughs" after the police commander, Major-General Sir Hugh Tudor and they were to become the main protagonist against the Irish Volunteers.

These units, due to their harsh treatment of the general population, had the effect of influencing anybody not already a sympathiser with the IRA of becoming one.

If the British Commonwealth can only be preserved by such means, it would become a negation of the principle for which it has stood.'

(Lionel Curtis, *The Round Table*.)

Irish playwright Sean O'Casey described a raid by the Tans on his tenement house in Dublin as follows:

'A raid!... Which were they – Tommies (British soldiers) or Tans? Tans, thought Sean, for Tommies would not shout so soullessly, nor smash the glass panels so suddenly; they would hammer on the door with a rifle-butt, and wait for it to be opened. No, these were the Tans... A great crash shook the whole house and shook the heart of Sean... A mad rush of heavy feet went past his door, to spread over the stilly house; for no-one had come from a room to risk sudden death in the dark and draughty hallway... yet Sean knew that the house must be alive with crawling men, slinking up and down stairs, hovering outside this door or that one, each with a gun tensed on the last hair, with a ready finger touching the trigger. He guessed that a part of them were Auxies, the classic members of sibilant and sinister raiders. The Tans alone would make more noise, slamming themselves into a room, shouting to shake

off the fear that slashed many of their faces. The Tommies would be warm, always hesitant at knocking a woman's room about; they would even be jocular in their funny English way, encouraging the woman and even the children to grumble at being taken away from their proper sleep.'

The attitude of the Black and Tans can be best be summed up by one of their own divisional commanders:

'Now, Men, Sinn Fein have had all the sport up to the present, and we are going to have the sport now. The police are not in sufficient strength to do anything to hold their own barracks. This is not enough for as long as we remain on the defensive, so long will Sinn Fein have the whip hand. We must take the offensive and beat Sinn Fein at its own tactics... If a police barracks is burned or if the barracks already occupied is unsuitable, then the best house in the locality is to be commandeered, the occupants thrown into the gutter. Let them die there – the more the merrier. Should the order "Hands Up" not be immediately obeyed, shoot and shoot with effect. If the persons approaching (a patrol) carry their hands in their pockets, or are in any way suspicious looking, shoot them down. You may make mistakes occasionally and innocent persons may be shot, but that cannot be helped, and you are bound to get the right parties some time. The more you shoot, the more I will like you, and I assure you that no policeman will get into trouble for shooting any man.'

(Lt. Col Gerald Brice-Ferguson Smyth, Lt. Col. *King's Own Scottish Borderers, Divisional Police Commissioner/Commander for Munster.*)

Accompanied by General Tudor who had recommended him for the post, he advocated these brutal measures while addressing the RIC in Listowel, Co. Kerry in south Munster, June 1920. His speech caused a Constable Jeremiah Mee to hand him his cap, pistol, belt and sword and call him a murderer. He ordered Mee's arrest on the spot, but nobody complied. After a similar speech in Killarney, five constables resigned.

On 17th July 1920, Smyth was shot dead in the Cork City and Country Club by six Volunteers led by Dan "Sandow" O'Donovan of Coolavokig, Co. Cork. Railway workers refused to carry Smyth's body.

According to one Irish observer:

> 'They, (the Black and Tans) *had neither religion or morals, they used foul language, they had the old soldiers' talent for dodging and scrounging, they spoke in strange accents, called the Irish "Natives", associated with low company, stole from each other, sneered at the customs of the country, drank to excess and put sugar in their porridge.'*

In the summer of 1920 the Black and Tans burned and sacked small towns and villages in Ireland, beginning with Tuam in County Galway in July, including Balbriggan, Templemore, Trim and Thurles among many others. Due to the ferocity of the Tans' behaviour and the atrocities committed, feelings, in Ireland, continue to this day regarding their actions, and are still despised in the island. The brutal retaliation against defenceless Irish villages and people sickened and disgusted most of the world.

The Tans provided Sinn Fein with a propaganda gift. Even the general public in mainland Britain, members of parliament and the British press, were appalled by what they considered scandalous methods, and condemned them accordingly. Prominent among the many critics was King George V, who, in May 1921, told the Chief Secretary's wife, Lady Margery Greenwood, '*he hated the idea of the Black & Tans*' (Dr John Ainsworth: *School of Humanities & Social Science, Queensland University of Technology*).

All this was to play a large part in England's eventual decision to negotiate. Both units were viewed by Republicans as an army of occupation because of their duties and actions. Arthur Griffiths, who became President of Dail Eireann estimated that, in the first eighteen months of conflict, British forces carried out 38,720 raids on private homes, arrested 4,982 suspects, committed 1,604 armed assaults,102 indiscriminate shootings and burnings in towns and villages and killed 77 people, including women and children.

CHAPTER 20

Independence or death. A country that is deprived of its independence cannot be regarded as other than a slave in the eyes of the world.

(Unknown)

In April 1920, Volunteers decided on cutting the humpbacked bridge over the Cross River at Summerhill, Athlone, removing the keystone – the motive being, should the Tan's lorry come along during the night, they would plunge headlong into the river. The task was given to stonemason Volunteer John Harney.

At this time, and acting on orders from GHQ that the rest of the fewer, less protected, or vacated barracks be burned, hundreds of barracks throughout Ireland were set ablaze and rendered unfit for the return of British Forces.

In following these orders, upon his return from incarceration in Galway jail, Seamus O'Meara ordered the destruction of all RIC barracks in the Brigade area of operations. Orders were followed up and over the Easter weekend the barracks were burned and destroyed at Meaghera, and Moyvoughly on Easter Saturday morning, and Brawny (Irishtown, Athlone), Bealnamullia, Creggan on the Moate Road on Easter Saturday night; to be followed by the Drumraney and Tang Companies which burned down Littletown Barracks.

Having been involved in the torching of the Bealnamullia barracks, Volunteer Denis Manning tramped across country to burn down Kiltoom barracks.

'In our area, Creggan and Brawny barracks were evacuated, and we burned both of these on Easter Saturday night 1920, in conformation with the rest of the country. This was a countrywide operation, and it was gratifying to read in the daily papers of the period about the destruction of these enemy posts.

It indicated that the Irish people were up and thinking again on the right lines. The RIC were always looked upon as the No.1 enemy of the people. They were of the people – being Irishmen – and it was understood by all that they were the chief weapon by which the British government maintained a hold on the country. This evacuation, though only a limited withdrawal, was the beginning of the end, and was a great blessing to us as it allowed us greater freedom of movement. The RIC were the eyes and ears of the British government through their hirelings in Dublin Castle.'

(Tom 'Con' Costello.)

The same night the Volunteers raided the Excise Office in Athlone. They knocked on the door which was opened by the caretaker, and he was captured and held. In a four-hour operation they removed books, correspondence, financial documents and records of the British administration in Athlone, from the office into the yard and having made a pile of them, set them alight and totally destroyed them. The raiders got away safely.

As 1920 progressed and the frequency of IRA attacks increased, the RIC continued evacuating their outlying outposts and concentrated their men in larger garrisons in the towns. They had eventually realised they could not hold these posts any longer or else they would lose them and the arms also.

In June 1920 the Volunteers acted as guards at polling stations and public meetings.

CHAPTER 21

We make war that we may live in peace.

(Aristotle)

In some active areas violent conflict actually resulted in a dramatic decline in the organisation's membership during 1920. This was not the case in Westmeath, where the membership actually rose from 882 to 962 and an extra company was formed.

In June 1920, in an attack on Clara RIC Barracks in County Offaly, Volunteer Patrick Seery from Cluin-Ui-Thaidgh in County Westmeath was wounded and died from his wounds. He was buried at Meadon outside Tyrellespass. The Corralstown Company, along with some Battalion and Brigade officers paraded at his funeral. It was expected that the RIC would interfere but they did not do so.

In July, an eighty-strong force from the Athlone Brigade mounted an attack on Streamstown barracks in an attempt to capture it. Waylaying two RIC on their way to Mass at Boher Chapel, Con Costello and Jim Tormey swapped clothing with them and approached the barracks demanding entrance. Unfortunately the occupants had been alerted and as the duo stepped up to the door, a constable rolled a grenade out through a loophole in the second story. Jim grabbed Con and dragged him out of the way before it went off. A bomb placed by the Volunteers on a windowsill failed to go off and the attack reverted to a forty-five minute gun battle. Finally, the attackers left before reinforcements arrived. The barrack was then vacated by the RIC who withdrew to Mullingar. Twenty-four hours later the Volunteers returned and burned it down.

To combat the escalation of violence in certain parts of the country, Sir Richard Greenwood introduced a Bill to the House of Commons on 2nd August 1920 for the suspension of trial by a jury in Ireland. It was passed by both houses of parliament and received royal assent. The new regulations on the Restoration of Order (Ireland) Act, over seventy in all, took effect from 13th August 1920 and were proclaimed in Ireland on 21st August, extending jurisdiction on all aspects of law and order to court-marshals and the internment of civilians. Under the Act, a captured Volunteer found guilty by a civilian court was liable to death by hanging and if tried under a courts-martial he would be executed by a firing squad. To enforce this new Act, Ireland was now garrisoned with tens of thousands of British troops and RIC, plus their paid snoopers. This force vastly outnumbered the Volunteers.

On 3rd August, a bicycle patrol consisting of five RIC was ambushed between Kilbeggan and Rochfortbridge by a large party of masked and armed men. Constable John Phelps was shot in the arm, but the police managed to fight off their assailants, wounding some of them in the process.

On 13th August 1920 the Unionists Anti-Partition League called a meeting in Dublin to petition the British Government, urging them to grant self-government to all of Ireland, in the hope of bringing about a stop to the imminent anarchy. From their pleas, it is obvious that the petitioners now saw dominion status as the only way Ireland could remain united with Britain, while satisfying the desire of the majority of the Irish people and ultimately maintaining peace. They declared:

'We urge his Majesty's Government that every month of delay in adopting this course renders the situation more dangerous and the chance of agreement more remote.'

On 16th August 1920 British forces burned buildings in Templemore as a reprisal for IRA Action. Meanwhile, to build up stocks of weapons the Volunteers purchased British Army Lee Enfield rifles from underhandedly profiteering British soldiers based in Athlone, as well as from deserters. However, this was not without risks. Joseph Kennedy of Athlone, the Adjutant of the Brigade, bought a Parabellum, the American made MC10 pistol fitted with a revolutionary suppressor or silencer from so-called 'Deserters.' They turned out to be spies sent to trap him. Luckily, he was sent to County Longford with dispatches and so escaped arrest.

Thomas Keaveney from Cloonchambers, Castlerea, Co. Roscommon who worked as a pawnbroker's assistant in Athlone was also a Volunteer and when British soldiers of the Athlone barracks, who were notorious for pawning things, would bring in their rifles to be pawned, Thomas would, at a later date make certain that the local volunteers received them. The practice of pawning weapons did not last long in the British military.

'...he (Thomas Keaveney) brought me one with fifty rounds of ammunition and after a lapse of fourteen days he arrived one evening with another which he had concealed under his coat. A party of R.I.C. under the famous Sergeant Craddock, who was afterwards shot in Athlone, was raiding the house at the time. Keaveney was coming up the avenue or lane to our house when he ran into this raiding party who were just leaving. They halted him and asked him his business. He replied that he was a relative of people who lived locally and that he came out here

*every Saturday to spend all day Sunday and Sunday night at a
neighbour's house to dance.*

*Sergeant Craddock ordered him to be searched for dispatches.
Keaveney opened his coat including his inner jacket, saying "I
don't know what you are talking about." I could hear all this
from where I was standing near my own door. In opening his
jacket Keaveney continued to conceal the rifle between his inner
and outer coats. They searched his inner pockets but did not
discover the rifle and let him go. Immediately they had left he
dumped the rifle over the hedge in case he met any more of
them. When the raiding party had cleared off I got the rifle
which was not damaged in any way.'*

(Michael McCormack, *Witness Statement 1503 to the
Bureau of Military History*).

Some of the RIC were extremely sadistic and none more so than
Sergeant Thomas Martin Craddock, a Roman Catholic and a native
of Co. Donegal. In his forties, he was unmarried with 25 years'
service, and based in Fry Place, Athlone. Craddock had served in
the Boer War where he appeared to have picked up some cruel
habits. In the early summer he led a group of his men to the home
of Volunteer Joseph Cunningham, who was president of the local
Dail Court, *'Joe was almost beaten to death and was a wreck of a man
afterwards.'* Later on they burned down Joe's house. He was left
permanently damaged by the beating he received.

The Volunteers had started to raid the mail trains and in a post
bag from one of the raided trains they found a letter from Craddock,
who had been transferred from Athlone to the reserve in Dublin
depot, addressed to the Head Constable in Athlone and outlining
a plan of action against them. For this he was transferred back to
Athlone, where his favourite pastime was to put a revolver to young

men's heads and threaten to shoot them. So, with action sanctioned by Michael Collins, eight-man sections waited in ambush positions in different parts of Athlone on four selected occasions.

Volunteers George Cosgrove of St. Columbas Terrace, Athlone and Sean Rattigan of Patrick Street, Athlone, were sent to scout the town for Craddock. However, on each date the wily Sergeant succeeded in eluding them. Finally, on the 22nd August, Craddock and Constable Denis Mahon were seen to go into Forresters Hall, Comrades of the Great War Club, an ex-soldiers' hall in King's Street by Sean Rattigan, who had scouted the town looking for him. When the pair came out at midnight, all eight guns of the ambush party were aimed at Craddock.

Jim Tormey fired first. The RIC man never got further than a few steps past the doorway when he fell, hit four times and mortally wounded in the abdomen. Tormey also fired three shots at Mahon but his gun misfired and the officer got away. Craddock was carried back into the hall and a few minutes after, he was removed on a stretcher to the Victoria Barracks hospital. He was evidently in dreadful agony. Before the arrival of a Doctor and a Priest, the injured officer had expired at 1 o'clock. At the inquest that followed the District Inspector said of him:

> 'He served faithfully for many years and to my own knowledge was a most upright and most noble minded man. He did his duty fearlessly and conscientiously. He was never known and I do not think any living human being could say that he ever wronged any person.'

Constable Mahon went on to make converts to Sinn Fein by beating people to booster his own courage. He pulled the archdeacon Of Saint Peter's Catholic Church out of his confessional box and threatened to shoot him.

On 24th August, Constable William Grier was held up in a Kilbeggan pub by three armed and masked men and relieved of his revolver and seven rounds of ammunition.

'About September 1920, an ambush party of military took place at Coosan. Information was received that a party of military about 40 to 50 strong had commandeered Cohen's motor launch and had gone up the river towards Lough Ree. James Norton, who lived at the Strand, Athlone, had seen them go aboard the boat in the early morning while it was still dark and, as such he thought they were Black and Tans as he could not distinguish between the uniforms. Norton told a girl, Miss Lily Mulvihill, who was a member of the Cumann na nBan, about this and asked her to tell the Volunteers. She came to me (Frank O' Connor of Coosan) and told me what Norton had told her. The brigade adjutant, George Manning, was hiding in the woods in Coosan at this time as were a number of others and some of the column, and we decided to attack them when they were returning. We presumed they had gone to raid the Islands in the Lough (Hare Island and Friars Island). *We mobilised a party of our men about 40 to 50 strong. We had a good few rifles, I would say nearly 20, and shotguns. We moved to and occupied a position on the river bank convenient to the "Thatch" public house at Hill Quarter, Coosan* (and the White Buoy in Shancurragh). *Scouts were placed on the hill tops* (at Ballyglass) *where they could observe the river towards and into the Lough and these men had runners or connecting files to us. About 3.30 in the afternoon we were informed that the boat was returning. When it got into the narrows of the river and broadside to us we could see that the*

deck was crowded with soldiers, not Tans. Seamus O'Meara was in charge of our party and he had ordered us beforehand to fire on the waterline of the boat. O'Meara had joined us just previous to the ambush and his idea was to sink the boat and deal with the occupants as they left it. The idea was ridiculous to think you could sink a launch that quickly by rifle and shotgun fire. A whistle blast was the signal for our men to fire at the men on the boat deck. Our first volley knocked out seven men – three officers and four privates were wounded. We kept up the fire and followed their boat down the river, moving from cover to cover along the river bank to about a quarter of a mile from the town. On firing our first volley the engine of the boat stopped, but started again in a matter of a few seconds.

The military had a Lewis gun on board and they opened up with this, but their fire was ineffective as they were too low down on the river and we were on the banks and their fire was going over our heads. We kept up fire on the boat moving from position to position as it sped down the river, but our fire was not effective and as we neared the town we had to call off the chase and they escaped. Some time prior to the boat coming into the ambush position, two soldiers from the garrison started to fish from a small boat in the river just opposite to us and we had to call them in and keep them prisoners until the ambush was over. We had no casualties.

Had our men been told to concentrate their fire on the men on deck instead of the waterline of the boat, the British casualties would have been much heavier. As it was, they never attempted to raid the islands again.'

(Frank O'Connor, *Witness Statement No: 1309 to the Bureau of Military History.*)

In May, the Volunteers once again started to raid the up and down mail trains in Knockcroghery and near Fassaugh, Moate Co. Westmeath, by taking over the signal box and station a few minutes before the trains' arrival. Two men then boarded the engine and three the mail van. They would take the post bags from the train and take them across the Shannon by boat to the home of Bernard Gaffey in Garrynagowna, also a base for the Athlone Flying Column. There, over the period of a week they would inspect the mail to gather intelligence for the Brigade. When sorted and marked with 'Passed by Censor,' the bags were taken back across the river and left outside Ballinahown Post Office. The value of this operation lay in the planting of fear in the minds of those who might be tempted to betray the Volunteers.

Sometimes the raiding of the mail trains resulted in ironic twists of fate. In the 3rd Battalion North area they had intercepted a letter from Captain Peake, commanding officer of the Stokestown garrison to his wife. In it he detailed his *'last will and testament'* as well as stating that all "Shiners" in the area were either locked up or had left the area. He mentioned Tommy Mason, Martin Fallon, and Sean Leavy by name, who was alive and living in Scramouge; he read the letter and sent it on to Captain Peake through the post office, signed with a personal notation that the Volunteers were glad to see he had his affairs settled up. Peake was later killed in an ambush at Scramouge. During this time, some railway workers in Westmeath refused to carry Crown Forces or their supplies and the Volunteers assisted by collecting for the dependants of the men dismissed from the railway for their attitude and actions.

Actions against the authorities continued to prevail throughout the month, especially with a big increase in the holding up and stealing of mails of which there were six cases. After the Restoration of the Order of Ireland Act and the increase of troops in Ireland, both Tans and regular army, the rebels were suffering mounting casualties and arrests.

There were no immediate arrests in the months of August and September in Westmeath, but October saw fourteen IRA men arrested. This resulted in a number of men going 'on the run', like George and his friend Jim Tormey, going underground to avoid capture by British forces. In doing so, they renounced all their material possessions except their arms and ammunition. They, along with their friend Kit McKeown, were to be 'on the run' until The Truce was declared. As the local RIC men knew the inhabitants in their district, the Volunteers were well known to them, and had their homes frequently raided but they always managed to be absent. The most dangerous place to sleep as a hunted man was in his own home.

George had a narrow escape when the military carried out a search of all the houses in Moate. Visiting the family home at the time, it was surrounded by armed soldiers in the night. With no way of escape, he got in-between his parents in their bed. He was lucky that it was British soldiers and not Tans who did the searching as they did not force them to get up and out of the house while it was ransacked. This left George and his fellow volunteers afraid to approach their own homes.

Raids on houses continued incessantly, and almost every village in Drum received a visit at one time or another. Many raids took place after nightfall and the residences of two Macken families, Malachy and Michael's were burned down and a further burning took placed at Michael Keena's residence in the same village. In September the Crown Forces raided a Sinn Fein Court in Athlone and arrested the judges, solicitors and witnesses.

When hounded by the Tans, the Volunteers were sometimes forced to bunk down in bogs, ditches and fields, hay barns and sheds. A favourite ploy was to find a field where a cow had laid down to rest and chase the animal away from her cosy nest; George and his comrades would then snuggle into the warm patch surrounded by tall grass, there hidden from the prying eyes of the Tans. The Boys spent many such nights sleeping under the stars.

This situation brought about a change in tactics by the IRA high command under Chief of Staff General Richard Mulcahy. As well as urban guerrilla warfare, he decided to organise the growing number of men 'on the run' into ASU's (Active Service Units), operating as Flying Columns on a hit-and-run basis.

The concept of the Flying Column was to use men 'on the run' from the authorities as an armed and versatile force to mount a guerrilla campaign to carry out ambushes, assassinations, kidnappings and raids and to make Ireland ungovernable, so forcing the British Government to the negotiation table.

The Flying Columns were the elite of the IRA and the units were manned by full-time volunteers who mounted attacks on Tans, RIC and their barracks and staged ambushes of army patrols and convoys. Besides this, they began a system of cutting off roads, making the movement of military vehicles and convoys very dangerous and difficult. This new incentive was to meet with great success for the IRA whose avowed aim became, *'We will strike at will – We will strike where we please.'*

CHAPTER 22

War is simple enough. Find out where your enemy is. Get him as soon as you can. Strike him as hard as you can, and keep moving on.

(Ulysses S. Grant)

'*In the month of September 1920 orders were received from General Headquarters that an Active Service Unit or Flying Column was to be organised in the Brigade area. And steps were taken immediately to select men for such a unit. Men who were in a position to leave home permanently and men "on the run" were selected. In addition the members of the Brigade and Battalion officers were automatically members of the column.*'

(David Daly, *Witness Statement No: 1337 to the Bureau of Military History*).

The Athlone Brigade Flying Column was formed in the home of David Daly, a member of the column. There were nineteen men in all. They were the 'makers and shakers' of the rebel forces in area. The rank and file made up of the following members:

George Adamson:	Vice O/C Athlone Brigade
Dick Birtles:	O/C 2nd Battalion (Drumraney)
Tom 'Con' Costello:	Vice O/C Athlone Brigade
Edward 'Ned' Dowling:	O/C 'A' Company 3rd Battalion (Summerhill)

Bernard 'Barney' Gaffey:	O/C 3rd Battalion (Summerhill)
Tom Halligan:	Capt. 'A' Company 3rd Battalion (Summerhill)
Pat Macken:	Capt. Moate Company 1st Battalion (Athlone)
George Manning:	Adjutant 1st Battalion (Athlone)
Brian Mulvihill:	Quartermaster 1st Battalion (Athlone)
Henry 'Harry' O'Brien:	Capt. Coosan Company 1st. Battalion (Athlone)
Francis 'Frank' O'Connor:	O/C 1st Battalion (Athlone)
Seamus O'Meara:	O/C Athlone Brigade.

Brigade and Battalion officers on joining the Column would take the rank of ordinary volunteer for that purpose. This arrangement allowed such officer's latitude to absent themselves from the Column when necessary to look after their Brigade and Battalion appointments. If allowed to take rank in the Column, they would not be able to perform the duties of their normal appointment. They were backed by Volunteers, who did not possess weapons, or were too young, who blocked and trenched roads to prevent mobile Tan patrols, cut telegraph wires, conducted intelligence work, carried messages and scouted.

Seamus O'Meara, a leading light in the struggle for independence in Westmeath and a great motivator of men, appointed Jim Tormey, who was arrested in April and released from Galway Jail on 19th October, 1920 as leader of the Flying Column because of his service, training and combat experience in the British army during the Great War.

A man of splendid physique, good appearance, military bearing and a commanding disposition, he looked like a British army, or an RIC, officer. However, he tended to attract attention wherever he went. All movements by the Volunteers were full of danger as described by Henry (Harry) O'Brien from Strand Street, Athlone, Captain of the Coosan Company in the Athlone Battalion and James (Jim) Tormey:

> '...were having tea at the Royal Hotel in Athlone in 1920, when we were spotted by the Auxiliaries, who had just entered the premises "generally the worst for drink." Both men exited through the back door, and started walking through the town north-easterly and parallel to the Main Street. As they neared Maguire's pub, one of the Auxies tapped Tormey on the shoulder saying, "We want you, big fellow." Both men dived in the door of the pub, O'Brien shot the Tan who threatened to capture Tormey, and, by running down around the south side of town and crossing the Shannon, he made good his escape.
> (Henry O'Brien, *Witness Statement No: 1308 to the Bureau of Military History*.)

For armament the Column had ten service rifles with about 20 rounds per rifle. They also had shotguns and cartridges filled with buckshot, along with revolvers of different calibres and grenades.

The Column's first billet was at Tobber, in stables belonging to the Parish Priest, Father McGee. For a couple of days it became a beehive of industry with men coming and going and bringing equipment and so forth. Food was bought and paid for out of Brigade funds, and the local people helped out. Some of the shopkeepers in Moate sent out supplies of bedding and clothing for the men, free of charge, when approached to do so by local Volunteers. The Cumman na mBan were most useful in this respect.

Though based in Westmeath, the Flying Column was later billeted in the Summerhill area, and took part in ambushes throughout adjoining counties of Longford and Westmeath. The local Battalion were required to provide security forces for them in the way of guards and scouts.

Volunteers Michael McCormack and Patrick Reddington constructed dugouts for the safe storage of arms and men:

'We received orders to compile a list of friendly houses who would be prepared to keep men "on the run" or billet members of the Column when the unit would be in the area. We also had to erect dumps to take arms and construct a dugout where men could shelter, and this we did. The principle dump was at Drumraney.

(Michael McCormack, Witness Statement No:1593 to the Bureau of Military History.)

Michael drew up a list of 'safe houses' and barns, stretching from Clonown to Curramore in Kiltoom, and from Mount Temple to Drumraney on the east side where, with country folk like the Tully family in Newtownflood, Drum and Athlone, and the Volunteers:

'...were well aware of the secret bunker which was built below the outhouses of Seamus O'Meara (Athlone Brigade O/C) business premises (butchers shop). This facility undoubtedly saved the lives of many local volunteers and others who sought refuge there during the early years of the struggle.'
(Gearoid O'Brien, Executive Librarian, Athlone Library – The Westmeath Independent.)

In answer to the activities, British troops poured into the area in an effort to curb Tormey's column. The Column, hard pressed, retired to the safety of the Slieve Bloom Mountains. As an old song says: '*…and to the Slieve Bloom Mountains came Jim Tormey's Flying Column.*'

The Cadamstown Company now had the honour of guarding Tormey's column for three weeks as they rested in the mountain. The Column then returned to engage in action with the British Forces. On 16th October, armed and masked men searched Athlone for wanted men. In the same month, Athlone barracks were bombed.

After this, 'E' Company of the 1st Battalion, Athlone Brigade received intelligence that a lorry load of police, travelling from Dublin to Athlone, was due to pass through Moate on Friday 22nd October 1920. On receiving this information, Jim Tormey and Seamus O'Meara scouted the Dublin to Athlone road for a possible ambush site. They found one at Parkwood, Clara, Co. Offaly, and took up positions at 3 o'clock in the morning, with the main force on the high ground on the west side of the road.

The weather was dry and mild. The site was on high ground a hundred yards from the Horseleap side of Murray's gate and McCormack's house in Parkwood. Two men with whistles were placed on the high ground on the Dublin side, where they had a full view of vehicles coming from the direction of Horseleap, to give warning of the approach of the police lorry. A further two men were put in position on the east side to deal with any police who might try to get out there.

No blocking of the road was attempted, as this was not feasible owing to the amount of traffic on the road and the fact the ambush party had no exploder to operate a mine. They aimed to shoot the driver of the lorry and bring it to a halt in the ambush position.

The main force took up positions on the south of the road, where they had the shelter of the hedge and some bushes, which formed a plantation; inside, eight volunteers armed with rifles. Six carried shot-guns and Jim Tormey, in command of the operation, had a revolver. Ammunition was limited to seven or eight rounds per man. The Volunteers, excluding Jim, George, and two other ex-British soldiers named Tommy Claffey and Bill Casey, were not experienced in the use of rifles, so a position was chosen close to the road nearly at point blank-range.

The regular police convoy consisted of two Crossley Tenders or small lorries, both fast and silent, well suited for carrying out surprise raids, as they could arrive at a selected spot without making any noise while approaching. Crossley Motors, a British company, produced the Crossley Tender model 20/25. It had room for eleven men, three in the front with the remainder facing each other on bench seats. Protection from the weather was by two hoods, one in the front and one in the rear.

The Volunteers made ready to deal with that number. However, between one and two o'clock in the afternoon the scouts signalled the approach of three tenders. These were preceded at some distance by a motor-car, containing police officers of high rank, which was unnoticed. The car passed through the ambush area unmolested and pulled up near the road from Marshbrook to Tubber, before proceeding to the RIC barracks in Moate. One Volunteer was restrained by Tommy Claffey from stepping out as the first tender appeared over the hill.

As the whistle sounded for the first volley, the men opened fire on a lone lorry of Tans. The driver was killed instantly, and the constable beside him fell to one side. The Volunteers thought the two were killed, but the second was only wounded in the leg. The tender lost speed and its occupants swayed forward. The vehicle ploughed into the hedge near Murray's gate. Unfortunately for the Volunteers, the camber of the road brought the tender to their side and gave its occupants, when they jumped off, full shelter of the hedge. The first lorry was all too quickly joined by three more.

The Column had unwittingly attacked a convoy of Black and Tans proceeding from Gormanstown in County Meath to Galway in the west. An eyewitness reported between twenty and thirty of them.

Two tenders pulled up, turned and escaped back to Kilbeggan. Why they did this remains unexplained. Two Tans, who sheltered on the off-side of the first tender, appeared, and Tommy Claffey fired twice at them without effect.

Other Tans crept along the grass margin in the shelter of the ditch until they reached a gap that gave access into the field. Further shots followed as some Tans got into the field.

Realizing that they had bitten off more than they could chew, Jim Tormey broke off the engagement and the Column withdrew, with no injuries. They made a successful retreat by commandeering a lorry belonging to Messrs. Goodbody of Clara, driven by Jim Mullins to nearby Ballymoney, County Offaly, and relative safety. They arranged for a boat to transport the men across the River Shannon where they billeted for two weeks.

In the attack, Constable Harry Briggs, a native of London, a driver of one of the three tenders involved, was killed and several constables wounded. Had the ambush been successful, it was intended to seize the lorries, arms and ammunition, put on the occupants' uniforms and drive into the police barracks in Moate. By this ruse, the Volunteers hoped to capture the building, which was protected by sandbags around the door, barbed-wire entanglements seven or eight yards deep on all sides and windows sheeted with bullet-proof steel.

Reprisals for this audacious act of defiance brought scores of

Black and Tans to the Moate area. Several houses were burned, and many of the people stayed out in the relative safety of their fields, rather than venture into their cottages. The surrounding area was now continually raided by enemy forces. In the weeks that followed, the commanding officers determined it would be wise to split up the column into smaller segments, each section scouting its own prescribed area and striking as the opportunity arose.

On 22nd Michael Burke of Athlone was wounded when the RIC fired on a group of civilians. Following this, on the 31st an attack was made near Kielty, Drum, Athlone, by Athlone Flying Column, when RIC Constable Doyle was wounded. In retaliation, on 1st November the Tans burned down the home of Michael Macken, Lisdillure, Drum. Michael was a Volunteer in the Drum Coy, 3rd Battalion, Athlone Brigade. At the same time, they burned down the Sinn Fein Hall at Crannagh, Drum, Athlone. Then, to the absolute delight of the Athlone Brigade, the British Forces had what is called a 'blue on blue' when they fired on each other in error, wounding three of their number.

CHAPTER 23

It is better to die fighting for freedom than to live a life in chains.

(Unknown)

On the morning of 2nd November 1920, Dick Birtles commanded an ambush party of twenty-three men armed with rifles and shotguns, the number of Volunteers as dictated by the number of weapons available. The section was made up from Volunteers of the Ballymore company along with members of the Drumraney and Tang companies, both attached to the 3rd Battalion. A local priest, Father Casey, gave them his blessing and absolution before they moved out to the ambush area. The ambush was sited in the Auburn area of County Westmeath on the main Athlone/Ballymahon Road:

> *We took up a position on one side of the road. The road at this point ran through a cutting and down to a bend. It was not an ideal position by any means as there was a lake in our rear, but better than the other side of the road. We hoped to get an enemy party coming from Athlone but prepared to meet them coming either way. For this purpose, two of the riflemen were stationed on either end or flank of our position with orders to shoot the driver of the leading lorry. We did not place any block on the road but relied on concealment and the ability of our riflemen to halt the lorries.*

After spending some time – five or six hours – in position, we heard lorries or tenders approaching from the Longford side and not from Athlone as we had hoped for. Our riflemen at that flank opened fire on the driver of the leading of the two tenders of police but missed him and killed the sergeant who was sitting behind him. The tenders drove on through our position and our men raked them with buckshot from the guns as they did so. Our home-made bombs were also thrown into the tenders, but for some reason, they did not explode this time.

It was noticeable that in the leading tender only a few police remained in a firing position; the others apparently knocked out and were down on the floor. There were only three or four police to be seen in either tender. One of our men – Volunteer Finn – was killed by a rifle bullet.

(Anthony McCormack, *Witness Statement No: 1,500 to the Bureau of Military History.*)

As two Crossley tenders carrying Black and Tans, on their way from Carrick-on-Shannon to Athlone to attend a court-martial, entered the ambush site, the section riflemen opened fire killing the driver of the first tender, believed to be a Tan named Larkin. Another man, in the cab, immediately took over the driver's position and drove the lorry, with all speed, through the ambush position.

The volunteers could not successfully disable the driver of the second vehicle with buckshot – the only weapon most of them possessed. Three hand grenades were thrown into the tenders but failed to explode. However, three other constables were wounded. Volunteer Seamus Finn, from Killeenbrack, lost his life that day. Only sixteen years of age, he was ordered to stay away; he disobeyed and paid for it with his young life. A memorial was erected to him at the site of the ambush.

There is no evidence that George was a member of the section under Dick Birtles in the action, but in a strange coincidence the ambush party was sited on land owned by Charles G. Adamson, believed to be an estranged relation of George, due to the conversion to the Catholic faith by George's branch of the family.

Charles Graham Adamson, aged 56 at the time of the incident, was born and raised at Auburn House, Glasson, a large estate property and 135-acre farm, which consisted of the entire town land of Auburn. He had inherited it from his father George. The following account seems to show Charles as a kindly man, but pro-authorities in outlook. The incident, recorded in his account book for the day in question, is as follows:

'2nd November (1920)

Had breakfast and went out to the potato field and started the boys picking up loose potatoes. After half an hour heard many shots in direction of Pigeons, afterwards two single shots. Heard motors coming. Told boys to run away as fast as they could. Another boy digging potatoes some distance away did not hear me and did not get under cover quick enough, started running too late and I believe was fired at. I hastened to the house to look after my family and called for them.

The maid told me that they had gone up the wood walk. I was going up after them when I met four armed strangers on my gravel. I went towards them and asked if there had been any casualties to the police and they said no. I asked if they had any, they said one and he is probably dead now. We went up to the wood walk and found the boy in extremis. The four knelt down and said prayers. I turned my back. After the body showed no signs of life, we had a consultation as to its disposal. I suggested putting him in my hall pending other arrangements.

They asked me to send for a priest. I sent my daughter on bicycle for priest and doctor. They carried the body and laid him in my hall and crossed themselves leaving. They gave me no directions as to the disposal of the body. Afterwards Father Coughran left and we all went to search to see if there were any more bodies in the wood but found none. There was a gun cocked and fully loaded. Fearing it might cause an accident I took the two cartridges in hall window and the Police took them away. Gave Father Kinahan a telegram to C.O. Man shot dead here. Afterwards he said he would rather stay here a while so I gave it to Doctor Clancy. At twelve we had tea.

After about an hour Police came into wood with revolvers. I walked up to meet them and said I had a dead man in the house. They took the dead man away. The ladies went down the avenue to talk to some soldiers. I waited to get bloodstains washed away. Soon all military and police left. Before leaving I told them that I was sure no one in the district were concerned in the raid. Attended the inquest next day and gave evidence.'

This was not the only action at Auburn during the "Troubles" as Charles recorded other activities, which he included in a subsequent claim for damages caused during the period 1921-1922. (Finian Corley: *Ambush at Auburn 1920 Journal of the Old Athlone Society 2003.*)

Volunteer Finn's body was taken to Athlone Military barracks. Having succeeded in identifying his body, a raid was planned on his family home looking for his brother and vowing they would shoot him when they got him. A friendly RIC constable called Woods, from Mullingar, cycled to the house of Volunteer Michael Murray of the Castlepollard Company, who lived in Ballynacarrigy, and told him that the Finn house was to be raided the following morning at a certain hour, and that Finn's brother was going to be shot. Michael immediately cycled to the Finn home and warned him to clear out, which he did. The following morning the house was raided, but young Finn was not to be found. His brother's body was eventually handed over to his uncle and his widowed mother, by the military, for internment.

It was reported that between four and five members of the RIC were wounded in the ambush. In reprisals, the military burned houses in Drum and Moore, including the farmhouse of John Flanagan, which was near the scene of the ambush and some out-offices of Doolan's of Meaghra, but the dwelling-house somehow escaped. The house of Ellen Lennon, the mother of four sons, from Crannagh, Summerhill, Athlone, was burned to the ground. They also entered two pubs in the town and four houses in the surrounding area and damaged them. Several men who they found on the roads locally were beaten up by the military and generally ill-treated, and around Meaghra, the people had to go into hiding to escape them. Then, on 3rd November 1920 British Forces burned down Athlone Printing works because the editor, McDermot Hayes, came out strongly against Crown and Tan actions. This left Athlone and district without a daily newspaper for over two years. The ASU (Active Service Unit) Flying Column, continued to travel back and forth across the River Shannon attempting ambushes in both County Westmeath and County Roscommon.

'It was backward countryside all along the Shannon bank; so during the struggle for independence, or The Troubles as we say, this was a favourite place for the boys "on the run". They moved back and forth from Carricknaughton or Clonown to Clonbonny and from Clonbonny back up to Ballinahown. As *there was no road into Lower Clonbonny there was no way the Black and Tans could pursue the lads with their lorries. One of my uncles used to stay out at night on the road listening for the Crossley Tender while the boys were sleeping. I only knew of one close shave; it happened when The Tans came in one morning through Kilgarvan Glebe from the Ballinahown direction. Con Costello from Killgarvan, (Athlone Brigade Officer Commanding) who was "on the run" himself, came down this way roaring to the boys that the Tans were coming. But they were too lazy to get out of bed and were almost caught. The Tans fired at them but they were able to escape across the Shannon. None of them were hit but the people who had been sheltering them got a bad going over with butts of rifles.'*

(Frank Hempstead & Geoffrey Foy: *Life in a Flood Plain of the River Shannon.*)

In November, the Tans 'besieged' Tralee in revenge for the IRA abduction and killing of two local RIC men. They closed all business in the town and let no food in for a week. In addition they shot dead three local people. On 14th November, they abducted and murdered a Roman Catholic priest, Fr. Michael Griffin, in Galway. His body was found in a bog in Barna a week later. The Tans sacked Cork city. On the night of 11th December 1920, the centre was burned out. These actions further incensed the IRA units around the country. On 15th November police barracks at Ballinagore, Coole, Crazy Corner, Fardrum, Lisclogher, Moyvore and Stoneyford were evacuated, thus weakening police control in the area which then came under IRA control. In the same month, Constable Larkin was shot dead, and Constable Ashcroft wounded in the arm in Athlone. Outside Moate, there was an attack on a Black and Tan patrol with the result that one was killed.

Such attacks became less feasible as the weakly fortified posts were abandoned, but the Westmeath Volunteers, unlike those of some other counties, continued to attack barracks after the Summer of 1920, with five or six such attacks happening after this time. Between July and December, there were six attacks in Kilbeggan. In a ten-month period to October, volunteer units throughout the country had destroyed 64 courthouses and destroyed or forced the RIC to evacuate some 492 barracks.

In December 1920 Athlone Brigade staff, which included George, had a meeting with Michael Collins in Dublin. By this time Collins, the Irish revolutionary leader and Director of Intelligence for the IRA, had become a legendary figure in the fight for an independent Ireland. He took a leading role in the Easter Monday 1916 Rising. On his release from Frongoch internment camp in Wales, his achievements were substantial. He arranged a 'National Loan'. Inland Revenue ceased to operate in most of Ireland, and the people encouraged to subscribe to Collins' Loan to set up funds for the young government and its army. It eventually reached £358,000 sterling. An even bigger amount, totalling $5 million dollars, was raised in the United States by Irish Americans, and sent to Ireland, to help finance the Republic. He organized the IRA and at one time led the government in the absence of de Valera, who spent most, if not all, of the 'Tan War' period in America.

The State of Northern Ireland was established on the 23rd December 1920, by the passing of the Government of Ireland Act 1920, the first step in the partitioning of Ireland.

Two months later Sir Nevil Macready, Chief of London's police, appointed Commander-in-Chief of British Forces in Ireland 1918-1920. He issued the December 1920 Proclamation of the death penalty for the possession of arms and explosives. In December 29th 1920, the British Government sanctioned official reprisals in,

Ireland – usually meaning burning property of suspected Irish Republican Army Volunteers, and their sympathisers. During this time, arrests of leading IRA officers never relented, and this seriously depleted their resources.

CHAPTER 24

Those who aim at great deeds also suffer greatly.

(Plutarch)

In January 1921, the British Labour Commission produced a report on the situation in Ireland, which is highly critical of the government's security policy. It said the government, in forming the Black and Tans, had *'liberated forces which it is not at present able to dominate'*.

A cooling-off period had occurred with no attacks upon R.I.C. in January, but attacks on crown forces continued hereafter, with two in February, three in March, five in April, six in May, six in June and four in July.

On 5th January 1921, Volunteer Anthony McCormack was captured outside Tang Chapel. He had gone to confession the previous evening, and while at Mass, the place was surrounded by a force of military and Tans.

At this time, January 1921, among other members of the Athlone Brigade interned in Ballykinlar concentration camp in Tyrella, Nr. Downpatrick, County Down, Northern Ireland, were Joe Tormey aged nineteen, brother of Jim Tormey, and Patrick Sloan a young married man from Mount Temple, Co. Westmeath. There were some 3,300 Volunteers in such camps throughout the country.

On arrival at Ballykinlar, after a three-mile-march, handcuffed and carrying their luggage, prisoners were placed in bare, corrugated iron huts with nothing to sleep on except damp straw. They found the camp regime to be brutal – with prisoners shot dead for minor infractions, such as standing too close to the barbed-wire fence that kept them pinned in.

So it was, on 17th January 1921, Joe and Patrick were walking towards the wire when an over-anxious sentry watching them decided they were planning an escape and shot them. They both died from shock and haemorrhage.

The military authorities claimed the young men were attempting to escape. Archival sources show this tragic episode is recorded simply as the guards had orders to shoot anyone approaching the wire, and no one doubted they were quite prepared to shoot. Their remains were brought home for burial – Joe Tormey to Moate and Patrick Sloan to Drumraney. The Tormey funeral took place from Moate to Mount Temple, and Sloan's to Drumraney. Both churchyards were crowded with military for the funerals; rifles and machine-guns peeped from every vantage point. It was a display of armed might but an unnecessary one, as there were no incidents.

It seems, on the death of his brother Joe, Jim Tormey wanted revenge against the Crown Forces for the shooting. His appeal to Command Headquarters for a retaliatory ambush was not sanctioned. So, he and George decided to take matters into their own hands and get even.

They immediately planned an attack for the Ballykinlar deaths on a number of policemen from Clonark RIC station in South Roscommon. They knew that on Monday 2nd February the police would travel to Athlone for supplies of ammunition, and they would be carrying the month's wages for the garrison at Cloonerk. It was decided to make the attack at Cornafulla, near Creggan,Co. Roscommon about four miles south west off Athlone. Jim ordered a mobilisation of local Volunteers west of the Shannon, where he was well known, to assist in the action.

On the morning of the day before the ambush Jim and George rowed across the River Shannon from Carrick-O-Brian, as both were marked men and could not risk travelling through Athlone, and made their way to Carricknaughton on the Roscommon side of Athlone. To their surprise and for reasons unknown, only two other members of the Flying Column were there to take part. The Roscommon Volunteers who joined them were cousins, and both named Tom Halligan.

Tom Halligan from Bogganfin Athlone was a Captain in the 3rd. Battalion Athlone Brigade and a member of the Athlone Flying Column, while his cousin Tom from Carricknaughton, Drum, Athlone, was also connected to the 3rd Battalion.

At the beginning of the day, the ambush plan was refined and preparations made. Then, the four volunteers travelled to Drum. Skirting the railway that evening, they met up with and had a brief conversation with a local man Larry McManus. Before parting, Jim told him he had been to Confession to Fr. Neary. At about 11 p.m. they stopped at the Higgins house in Curryroe where they had some bread and milk. When the group entered the kitchen, young Margaret Higgins became frightened with the sudden invasion into her house. A tall young man in uniform came over to her and said, *'Don't be alarmed, we only want something to eat.'*

Before the group left the kitchen James Tormey came over to Margaret again and apologised for having frightened her and said, *'When this war is over, I will come back and talk to you.'*

Moving on, they stayed overnight at the 'safe house' of Sarah Hughes at Collagorriff. As the morning sun rose higher in the sky, the four men tramped across the fields and the moor area of Crannaghmore, where they spoke to Patsy Donlon who was tending to some pits of potatoes in his tillage field, no doubt checking with Patsy for any enemy forces. They continued on to Garrynagowna. When the ambush party reached Cornafulla on the Ballinasloe-Athlone road, about noon, they learnt that three policemen had already passed, in the early morning, on their way to Athlone and would return in a few hours. So, about 12.30 and still waiting for the local men to mobilise, they took up a position a hundred yards behind a fence at Richard Bigley's field in Creggan, and waited for their prey.

Visibility was good as they waited patiently for the policemen to return from Athlone with their ammunition, provisions and wages, which they had collected for their headquarters. About ten minutes after three, eight to ten policemen on bicycles suddenly appeared round the bend and cycled past the ambush party. Jim Tormey, realizing the party were too strong, decided not to attack but let them go by. After the police had passed by, for some unknown reason, probably the murder of his brother in Ballykinlar Camp, he rose up and opened fire.

The police scrambled into the roadside ditch and began to return fire. The Volunteers opened their attack, but in less than a minute, when it was too late, the attackers saw the police being followed by fourteen Tans and regular soldiers, also on bicycles. This rear party halted and deployed down a side road or *boreen* which ran at right angles to the main road and outflanked the small party.

During the gun battle that followed Tom 'Leix' Halligan shot the cap off one of the police, and immediately afterwards, the foresight was shot off his own rifle. Witnesses stated that rifle-fire could be heard from a distance of two miles from the scene of the ambush. Local men John Goodde and Patrick Gavin both returning from Athlone arrived at the Taylorstown road as the shooting began. They dismounted from their cart and took cover in the roadside ditch. While there, a policeman removed his cap and showed them the hole created by a bullet passing through it – gesturing to Gavin at the same time, '*This is what your policy is about.*'

The Volunteers soon realized that they were hopelessly out gunned. Immediately, Jim Tormey signalled a retreat to avoid being surrounded and commenced a withdrawal action. Jim was first to move and retreated to a ditch in the rear of his party, to be followed by George. The Halligans were the next to move to new positions while Jim and George supplied covering fire.

They dropped back by two's to successive covering positions until the retirement was completed. This alternate manoeuvring, called 'pepper-potting' in the British Army, ensued for nearly half an hour. During this action, gunshots resounded over the fields for several miles in all directions.

Under cover fire by Jim Tormey, the other three got back safely. Meanwhile, unseen, one or two policemen moved down the side road near to where Jim Tormey was; as he took up a vantage position standing on Richard Bigley's plough (as told by Joe Bigley), one of their bullets aimed at George and the Halligans, hit Jim in the head, through the left cheek, as he stood up. It was a chance shot but an unlucky one.

It was said that no one saw him fall, neither his companions nor the police. When George crossed the hedge, he found him to be breathing his last and he passed away within minutes

Seeing that there was nothing he could do for his 25-year-old best friend, and with Tom 'Pat' Halligan covering their retreat, the remaining trio succeeded in getting clear back to Clonown. Not knowing the reason for the ceasefire, the Crown forces suspected that the attack, by just four men, might be a ruse to draw them into the open field where a more numerous group could pick them off.

While the shooting was going on, many people were returning from the pig fair which was held in Athlone earlier that morning.

Patrick Shine of Kielty took the situation in hand where he advised and directed many cart drivers to travel up the Lisdillure road and make their way back to the main road to Cornafulla, thereby avoiding the site of the ambush.

However, one such cart driver, Jack Caulfield from Derryneil, accompanied by his sister, refused to take advice about the detour. The couple arrived at the scene of the ambush just as the shooting ended. Seizing the opportunity, the Tans commanded Caulfield to dismount from his cart and at gunpoint directed him to cross the open field towards the spot from where the gunfire had come. But Caulfield outsmarted them and did not return. Instead, he hastened across the fields and through the bog to Cornafulla, and his home in Derryneil.

This chance manoeuvre was most likely the reason why the crown forces decided to withdraw and return to Athlone without making any advance against their enemy that afternoon – apparently unaware they had shot Tormey or too frightened to search the area, where they would have found his body.

Meanwhile, George and the Halligans dashed through the fields hoping to seek refuge in Bernard Gaffey's house, in Garrynagowna. Gaffey O/C 3rd Battalion and Volunteers from Gorry from the Summerhill Company had heard the shooting, and ran to their dump, got some shotguns, and rushed to the join in the action.

As it happened, they were soon to meet up with the ambush party. Then, after a briefing by George the new group decided to risk a return to the ambush site, on the Roscommon side of Athlone in the Clonark area, that night to recover Jim's body from the field where he died. They didn't want his body lying unattended in the field, waiting for the Tans to mutilate it. So, George, the two Halligans, Battalion Commander, Brian Gaffey, John Bohan, Eddie and Michael Cunniffe, John Harney, Mike

Hogan, Mike Hunt and Tom Tully undertook the dangerous mission of returning to the scene, not knowing whether or not the Tans may have remained lurking in the vicinity. The group were successful in recovering Jim's body and his weapon.

> *'We first carried Tormey's body to the nearby stream and then, using rifles as bearers, proceeded crouched between the banks of the stream for about one hundred yards, then somebody brought a door which they had got from a nearby out office in Taylorstown. On this the remains were carried as far as Tom Henry's at Togher, where a pony's cart was procured and which we pushed as far as Clonown Church. Here the remains were handed over to the unit members in Clonown under the leadership of Bill Fallon'* (Tom Tully).

(Liam Fox, *War of Independence in Drum 1916-1922*).

The group had only been gone from the ambush site about twenty minutes when the Cornafulla area was searched and raided extensively by reinforcements of the Crown Forces from Athlone, but they made no arrests.

The body was taken by cart from Clonown to the river Shannon and brought across at night to Clonbonny on the Westmeath side, where it remained overnight in an isolated shed in an unfrequented bog. Next day Seamus O'Meara made arrangements for a coffin and a burial habit for Jim, which was supplied by a friendly undertaker in Athlone. Jim was laid out, surrounded by lighted candles, and attended by ten Volunteers, who recited the rosary. George, in looking for the potent man he had known and loved as a brother, would have been unable to find him in the shell made of bones and sickly flesh.

The following night the coffin was brought down the river

Shannon on a 'cot', which is a flat type of boat used to carry hay and turf, on its mournful journey, to be buried in the old cemetery of the Seven Churches in the ancient monastic site of Clonmacnois in the County of Offaly. There a grave was dug, and ten of his former comrades laid Jim Tormey to rest amid the quiet and lonely ruins of 'St. Ciaran's city fair'. This fine monastery, the burial-place of many of the kings of Connaught and Tara, was reduced to a ruin in 1552 by the English garrison in Athlone.

The police later learnt one Volunteer was killed in the ambush, and a search of local cemeteries began. On Sunday, five days after the clash, the fresh grave in Clonmacnois was discovered (it would appear that an informant was at work here). On Tuesday 8th February, Cattle Fair Day in Athlone, the coffin was dug up and taken on a lorry to the Military Barracks in Athlone, under a guard of soldiers singing bawdy songs.

Some form of inquest or inquiry was held in the barracks. The breastplate of the coffin inscribed with his name, and the words *Killed in Action, 2nd February, 1921* left the Crown Authorities in no doubt who Jim Tormey was. The body had a wound in the left cheek. A detachment of the military was sent to the Tormey home in Moate where his aged father and uncle were brought in to identify the body. After accepting recognition, they were told they could reclaim it, and on the following day Jim was buried in Mount Temple cemetery next to his young brother Joe, a double loss for the grief laden Tormey family, as there was just three weeks between the deaths of the two brothers.

George's boyhood friend and comrade Jim Tormey had finally run out of luck. A truly brave man, he had survived the carnage of the Great War and many other hair-raising incidents to finally die in his own native land. One can only imagine the devastation felt by George at the tragic loss of his best pal from whom he had become inseparable.

For close on two years, they had shared the rigours of life 'on the run' living together in barns, ditches and hides, along with the 'white knuckle' moments of combat. He would have known that he would never have another friend like Jim. In a day of bitter memories, the world must have seemed a very dark place indeed. The leadership of this gallant soldier would not only be missed by George, but all of Jim's comrades in the Flying Column. Tom Moore, of Moate, composed a poem on the tragic affair and concludes:

'Through darkness of that wintery night we bore his body to Clonown.
Many's the prayer we said; many's the tear dropped down.
We waked him in a humble shed – no vanities did him surround.
The turf-boat was his funeral bier; the wreaths – turf piled round.
In Clonmacnois of holy fame we laid his body down to rest,
With no hoary scroll to tell the name of one him they dearly loved the best.
Alas! The Tans got on the scent; their eyes to wonder o'er...
When tired of gloating on their prey, reluctantly they gave him over,
An' now Mount Temple he sleeps 'neath a mount of Irish clover.'

In a reprisal for the Cornafulla ambush, the military burned down the house of William Nicholson and burned his neighbour Naughton's haystack. Following these incidents a series of ambushes and raids were carried out in Athlone, Castlepollard and Killbegan in retaliation. The Gaffey home was also raided by the Tans, where both Brian and his brother Paddy were dragged from the house and beaten so severely that Brian died from his injuries the following August 1921. Paddy escaped from his captors as the Tans were leading the brothers into captivity.

The Tans left no stone unturned in their attempts to capture

Volunteers, to the extent that on the 6th February 1921, they raided the Drum Church, Drum, Co. Westmeath, during the Mass. An unknown voice, from the back of the church interrupted the service with the words: '*The Tans are coming, if anyone wants to leave, leave now.*'

The Rev. Fr. Neilan, C.C. who was the celebrant of the Mass, advised the congregation to continue with the observance of the Mass. Some men were seen to leave by the sacristy door. The Tans did arrive and interviewed everyone in the chapel. (Patrick Kenny, Johnstown, Drum-3rd Battalion Athlone Brigade.)[5]

On 20th February 1921 Volunteer Joe Morrissey was killed in Athlone. On the same day the Flying Column made a successful attack on police barracks at Ballymahon. The column now moved on to Coosan and it was a full-time job now avoiding contact with the large enemy forces which were operating in the Area. The Column was in none too good shape – some of the original members were still absent from it and a lot of others had joined it. The reinforcements were men who were compelled to go 'on the run' and they had attached themselves to the Column. There was no effective armament for them. It was more of a gathering than a Column. After Jim Tormey's death Seamus O'Meara had taken charge of the Flying Column personally and his feelings at this time were recorded in his Witness Statement as follows:

---

[5] Many years after the War of Independence ended, Seamus O'Meara in referring to George, Jim and his brother Joe, in his Witness Statement to the Bureau of Military History recorded that '*sad to relate, their graves are grossly neglected, being covered with weeds and dirt. There is no monument or anything to mark the spot*'. Since then a stone has been erected in their honour. However '*sad to relate*', their unmarked graves are still covered with weeds and dirt; in fact, the whole cemetery is in a disgraceful condition.

'At this time our men were getting much out of hand and were doing things without the sanction of higher authority. About a week after Jim Tormey's death, some of them undertook, without authority to stage an ambush in Athlone. It now became clear to me that discipline had to a great extent been lost and that things were getting into a dangerous state when individual officers and Volunteers were taking on operations of their own accord without authority or co-operation of their headquarters. This, I could foresee, would end up in a big lot of young men being arrested, some of them under arms and suffering the consequent death penalty.

I could also see what arms we had being lost and the collapse of the movement in our area. I gave the matter considerable consideration and concluded that the best course was to write to G.H.Q. In Dublin, and place the whole matter before them. This I did, and in my report I asked that a reliable and suitable officer be sent down by them to take charge. I said in my report that I would be prepared to fight in any grade or position under this officer and I tendered my resignation as Brigade O/C.'

(Seamus O'Meara, *Witness Statement to the Bureau of Military History.*)

Acting on O'Meara's report to Dublin, a Simon Donnelly, who had escaped from jail, was sent down from G.H.Q. Dublin, on an inspection and organisation mission and called a meeting of the Brigade Council.

At this meeting O'Meara said that he wished to relinquish the command of the Brigade and he was allowed to do so and Tom Costello was now made Brigade Commander with George Adamson as Vice Commandant.

There were no changes to the Battalion staff. No one was appointed to command the Column definitely. It was arranged that where the Column was operating or billeted in a Battalion area, the O/C. of that Battalion would command it and, should it go into another Brigade area, the last O/C would continue to command. This arrangement had one advantage in that each Battalion Commandant knew his area and the Volunteer officers in it.' (David Daly, Witness Statement to the Bureau of Military History.)

David Daly was followed by Gerald Davis, County Organiser from GHQ in Dublin who noted:

'There was no real active service unit or flying column in the brigade area. The brigade organisation was in a pretty bad state. There had been a brigade column organised in the area and they had carried out a few ambushes and had lost a few men killed. Following the intense activity after those incidents, the column had got scattered and disorganised. The Athlone area was a very difficult one to operate in.

The country is generally flat and boggy and there are no mountains. Athlone was always a strong enemy garrison centre and the people in the town were none too friendly disposed towards us. I suppose this applied to all garrison towns. The people in the country, however, were generally all right and, with occasional exceptions, could be relied on.'

(Gerald Davis, Witness Statement to the Bureau of Military History.)

George and Gerald Davis, back in action together again after their ill-fated run in and wounding with the two Tans in the barnyard at Carricknoughton, had another 'close shave'. Along with volunteer Ned Dowling, O/C of 'A' Company 3rd Battalion (Summerhill), they just missed a round-up by Crown Forces, as Gerald Davis relates:

> 'After consultation with the Brigade O/C, when I was fit again, I decided to go to the Drumraney area and try to get some activity under way there. This decision was taken on a Sunday night and the following morning there was a big round up of the area where we were staying which was in a house near the Shannon. It was the Brigade O/C. who gave us the warning that the Tans were all round the place. I had a Colt revolver, but I had only three rounds for it. Adamson had no arms and neither had the other man, Dowling, who was also with us. By the time we got out of the house they were practically on us. We made a dash for the Shannon and, fortunately, there was a rowboat at the bank and we three jumped into it.
>
> Dowling and I took the oars and proceeded to row in the direction of Athlone. This was a lake part of the river and there was an island between us and the other shore. We rowed along keeping fairly near the bank. When we were gone a couple of hundred yards a bunch of Tans arrived at the bank which we had left.
>
> They looked at us for a while and then started to fire at us. I shouted to Dowling to row like hell. I don't know what happened, but when we started to pull hard, he pulled the boat into the bank.
>
> Apparently he was not keeping in rhythm with me. We had to leave the boat and wade through the river up to our waist and get on the same bank as the Tans were on. There was a slight

rise in the ground here which obscured us from their view temporarily. When we had crawled up on the river bank, they could see us and they again started firing at us. We ran for about a mile across the flat country with no cover, but the Tans had given up the chase and we got away safely. Adamson was not in too good form after his recent illness, (having been shot through the lung) *but he had been a cross-country runner in his earlier years and this stood to him now.*

After this round-up, I left Adamson and proceeded to Drumraney with a Volunteer named Casey. Having contacted Dick Birtles O/C of the battalion in that area, we proceeded to try and carry out some operations in that area. There was a village called Ballymore with a barracks housing a garrison of R.I.C. and Tans in that area. A patrol from this barracks came out nightly and patrolled the area. A Battalion meeting was called and plans were made to ambush this patrol, but, unfortunately, on the night before the ambush was fixed to take place, there was a big round-up in the area by enemy forces and I was caught. The whole area around where we were staying was surrounded. Casey was also caught, but was not held by them. He was a country-man and looked the part, whereas probably I did not. I dumped my gun before I was captured, as I only had three rounds for it, and that was of no use. I was detained and brought to the, military barracks in Athlone.

(Gerald Davis, *Witness Statement to the Bureau for Military History.*)

Gerald was arrested and by mid-May 1921 and was a prisoner in Athlone barracks. There, he was identified by one of the Tans from the shoot-out in the barnyard, at Carricknaughton, when he and

George were wounded. Gerald was sentenced to life imprisonment in Mountjoy Gaol in Dublin from where he escaped carrying a smuggled gun, and clothing. Gerald would later become a doctor in the new National Army.

CHAPTER 25

*The object of war is not to die for your country, but to make the
other bastard die for his.*

(General George Patton)

All the while, the local volunteers continued to stock-up on arms
and ammunition. By the Spring of 1921 they had acquired an
impressive stockpile of Martini, and .303 Lee Enfield rifles and
Webley service revolvers, acquired by raids on homes of retired
British Army officers. In a unique attempt to gain arms, Thomas
'Toby' Mannion and Tommy 'Tom' Martin, both from Barry Beg,
The Hill of Berries, Kiltoom and Volunteers in the 3rd Battalion
The Athlone Brigade, dressed up as a courting couple and disarmed
the double sentries on the Hall's (railway) Bridge leading westwards
out of Athlone.

> 'In April 1921, a number of young men not in the Volunteers
> went to the rifle ranges outside Athlone and destroyed the
> apparatus in the ranges including telephones and telephone
> cables. These men were subsequently taken into the Volunteers.
> In the latter part or 1920, and principally in 1921, the enemy
> carried out a number of large scale round-ups and, as a result
> quite a good few of our men had been arrested and interned.'
>
> (Frank O'Connor, Witness Statement No: 1309 to the
> Bureau of Military History.)

The big 'round-up' took place in 1921 when the whole country was saturated with the army in search of Volunteers. All out-houses were searched and many of these wanted men arrested, whilst others had narrow escapes and had to go 'on the run'. Local spies, in the employ of the Crown Forces, played a large part in providing information and intelligence on the whereabouts of the Volunteers and their activities.

> 'There was a man named Maher who was an ex-British officer living in Irishtown. He had a wooden leg, but travelled extensively throughout the country. He was under suspicion of spying for the British for a long time, and we had been keeping him under observation. He was arrested by George Adamson and Ned Doolan in Carrickbrien and court-martialed and sentenced to be shot. He had a small pension from the British Government, but claimed that he lived principally by begging, but our information, which was backed up by the evidence of the men who had been keeping watch on him, was that he was never known to have done any begging. He was found guilty and sentenced to be shot. He was shot and his body was thrown into the Shannon. We did not want his execution to become known so as to avoid reprisals by the enemy on Carrickbrien and that was why his body was given to the river. We forgot about the wooden leg and this kept the body afloat in the river where it remained for a considerable time. It was then hauled in and buried on the bank of the river by some of our men. I personally took charge of the execution party.'
>
> (Seamus O'Meara, *Witness Statement to the Bureau of Military History*.)

Following this, at Kilbeggan on 2nd March, a military dispatch rider was held up and relieved of his motorcycle. The machine could well have been the one used by Patrick 'Patsy' Rattigan, another close friend of George, who served as a dispatch rider for the Athlone Brigade. He was an excellent horseman, knew almost every inch of his home county. He would leave Athlone daily at 3 p.m., making the ten-mile trip to Moate to collect a motorcycle for the carrying and delivery of brigade dispatches.

His brother Sean had some trouble when travelling to Moate with confidential documents for George. British troops had received intelligence about the operation and hoped to intercept the messenger. However, because of his detailed knowledge of the lie of the land between Mount Temple, where his mother Margaret Claffey hailed from, Drumraney where his aunt Carthy lived, and Moate, along with other safe-houses en-route, he made it to Moate, and was given food, shelter and refuge by the Sisters of Mercy. His luck ran out in March 1921 when he was captured and imprisoned in Athlone Barracks. In an April 1921 raid on the Great Southern and Western Railway, George's previous place of employment, the Volunteers seized telephone batteries and cables necessary for the construction of bombs.

Another example of the thuggish and murderous *modus operandi* of the Tans occurred on May 14th 1921. They entered a public house and arrested young John P. Greene, a university student, who had no connections with any nationalist groups. Taking him outside, they made him walk out to sea, then fired shots at him. Then, wounded in the back and the neck, he was made to stand against the sea wall while they feigned his execution. Then, they beat him with their batons and let him go.

CHAPTER 26

Never interrupt your enemy when he making a mistake.

(Napoleon Bonaparte)

The Ireland of June 1921 was an island gripped by a war which had reached its zenith.

> *On the 11th June 1921*, one *of our men – Michael Hunt* [a member of the party that recovered Jim Tormey's body from Cornafulla and an active dispatch messenger with the Summerhill unit carrying messages to other units during his work on the railway] *was arrested while taking dispatches at the railway station in Athlone from the guard or driver of the mail train. The Tans followed him into the lavatory on the station premises and held him up and found the despatches under his coat. The forces who arrested him were composed of military and Tans. Hunt was taken to the military barracks where he was used as a hostage on lorries going out on raids and so forth. They made him dig his own grave in the barracks grounds and he was thrown into drains and beaten in an effort to get information from him. Hunt was eventually court-martial and sentenced to three years penal servitude. He was released in the general release in January 1922.*

(Patrick Lennon, *Witness Statement to the Bureau of Military History*.)
(Hunt was incarcerated in Ballykinlar Camp in Northern Ireland.)

In the Athlone district the IRA had been recently informed that Major-General Thomas Stanton Lambert, Commanding Officer of the British Army 13th Brigade garrisoned in Athlone with responsibility for Co. Westmeath, along with the General Officer Commanding the Dublin Brigade, were in the habit of going to a house near Coosan named Midges to play tennis. With this in mind the local IRA set up an ambush. The ambushers, *'about fourteen men'* in total, all disguised, were armed with revolvers, rifles and shotguns.

They were led by Captain John J. Elliott of the Tubberclare Company of Volunteers. The purpose of the ambush was to kidnap Lambert and hold him hostage to use as a bartering tool with the British for the recently captured County Longford, IRA leader, Sean MacEoin. MacEoin's capture, in March 1921, was a serious blunder by the Mullingar Volunteers. He was returning to his area of operations from a mission to headquarters in Dublin, travelling down to Mullingar, Co. Westmeath, by train to attend an IRA meeting. The local volunteers had been informed that it would be searched upon arrival as he was a *'marked man'*, and they were instructed to stop it before Mullingar at the Downs and get MacEoin off, and spirit him away to safety. Although the battalion officer who received the orders was arrested the night before the operation, the information still managed to reach the local IRA Company, but they didn't act on them.

> *'Mullingar railway station was bleak and shadowy, as the late train from Dublin that night drew into the platform. It was 1921- there was a party of the R.I.C. awaiting the train. They went along the carriages, taking out male passengers and lining them up on the platform to be searched and bullied and questioned. It was a familiar happening. Ireland was at war, albeit unrecognised. One man stood out in the line of*

unfortunate passengers, a young man of powerful physique and handsome, clever features. He gave his name as Smith from Aughnacliffe, travelling to Edgeworthstown. One of the uniformed men with the rifles at the ready peered closer. It was pure chance that he had a vivid memory of a strong, handsome face. 'Are you not John McEoin from Ballinalee?' he asked cutely, warily, knowing but too well that the man before him was no other. A buzz of excitement. Handcuffs snapped on. Surrounded by an escort of some forty policemen, MacEoin was marched off the platform, bound for the detention cell in Mullingar Barracks. The procession of policemen and prisoner marched along steadily. And then, at a turn in the roadway, the handcuffed man made a run for it and after a brief chase he was shot and captured on Mary Street.'

(John Mageean: *The Story of Sean MacEoin* (Man of the People) 1945.)

An IRA intelligence officer in the Mullingar brigade emphasized how grave this insubordination was, '*an event that affected the entire movement and that may have damned the Mullingar company ever since*'.

GHQ was furious at the incompetence and ordered MacEoin to be rescued at all costs; on no account were the military, police and civilian witnesses be allowed to reach Dublin. Thus, a Brigade operation was mounted in which Seamus Maguire, Brigade O/C personally took charge. He decided to lay an ambush on the main Dublin Road at Griffinstown for the purpose of releasing MacEoin.

About fifty or sixty men were mobilized from the area. They had fifteen to sixteen service rifles, all the property of the Mullingar Battalion, and the remainder had shotguns and revolvers. A concrete mine was placed in the road by the Brigade Engineer as the Volunteers took up position behind a fence on the roadside and in the ruins of some old buildings. They were there at about 5 o'clock in the morning, awaiting the enemy to approach.

The site selected was a good one, and probably the best in the area. The Volunteers depended on the explosion of the mine, and the first rally to make the enemy surrender. If all went wrong, they were prepared to fight to the death or surrender when their ammunition gave out. All was in readiness when the mine was accidentally exploded.

It went off in a terrific explosion, which blew a large hole in the road and felled a tree. The sound could be heard in Edenderry many miles away. This put paid to any ambush, and Maguire ordered the Volunteers to withdraw and disperse to their own areas, which they did without further incident. As it happened, the British was wise to the fact that attempts would be made at a rescue, so prisoner and witnesses did not travel that way from Longford, as they had taken an alternative, circular route to the city, travelling via Athboy and County Meath to Dublin, thus outflanking the ambush position on a wide scale. Meanwhile, owing to increased IRA activity on his patch, Major-General Lambert imposed a strict curfew on Co. Westmeath:

'All persons shall remain indoors between the hours of 22.30 hours and 05.00 hours and that within the Urban Districts of Athlone and Mullingar, all persons shall remain indoors between 23.00 and 05.00.'

On 29th June 1921, two days after releasing this statement, Lambert and his friend Colonel Challenor and their wives were travelling by car from Athlone towards the Midges house, outside Coosan, to play tennis. On a quiet road near Benown, they found their path blocked by a dozen armed men. This was the ambush set up by Captain John J. Elliott and the Tubberclare Company of Volunteers.

Elliott had been instructed to make use of a temporary road block, such as a farm cart which could be pushed out at the last minute. However, he failed to do so. Seeing the ambush ahead but no roadblock, Lambert, who was driving, in a state of panic, accelerated instead of stopping. At this the ambushers opened fire with their revolvers, rifles and shotguns. The car managed to get through the hail of bullets and carry on a distance further. The ambushers immediately fled the scene. The Major-General and Mrs Challenor were critically wounded, Mrs Challenor receiving severe facial injuries.

All four passengers were rushed to Athlone hospital, where Major-General Lambert died at nine o'clock that night. Lambert's assassination met with outrage and bitter indignation among the British forces, and there was an immediate cry for revenge among the ranks.

According to Tom 'Con' Costello:

> *'Military activity (British) now became intense, and they combed the countryside, including the islands on the Shannon.'*

Within a week social order rapidly broke down in the Glasson/Moydrum district, and martial law was rigorously enforced. In the meantime, the Black and Tans were tasked with seeking out the perpetrators of Lambert's murder.

The majority of IRA Volunteers in the Westmeath of 1921 came from farming backgrounds – farm labourers. This saw the Tans focusing their search for Volunteers and their arms in many farmsteads around south Westmeath. Frustrated by the lack of information they were receiving, they turned to reprisal tactics.

The month ended with the burning of the Ballymore Courthouse in Co. Westmeath by the Volunteers.

CHAPTER 27

You can discover what your enemy fears most by observing the means he uses to frighten you

(Eric Hoffer)

In the early curfew hours of Saturday 2nd July, at about 2 a.m., a number of masked men (estimated at twelve) believed to be Tans, carrying revolvers and wearing trench coats and tweed caps, raided and with the use of petrol, burned five farmhouses in the Hillquarter, Coosan district belonging to Thomas Duffy, Thomas Wansboro, Thomas Farrell, Mrs Coghlan and Patrick Moore, and Bill Concanon's haystack. Having been roughly handled by these strangers, the now homeless farmers and their families were left to watch their houses go up in flames. As if they hadn't caused enough damage, the Tans also set fire to their victims' outhouses and haystacks. After this, they went to Mount Temple, where they burned another farmhouse belonging to a Mrs Hennaly whose son was in prison for IRA activity. The homeless families were described as *'all hard-working, industrious people that took no part in politics.'*

These new methods harked back to The Boer War in South Africa, where, in 1900, British General Lord Roberts gave orders to burn all homes and farms in a 10-mile radius of attacks by the Boer Commandos, the British being of the opinion the commando could not operate in the area without at least the knowledge, if not the active co-operation, of the local residents. As the policy expanded, the British began to burn the farms and crops and kill the livestock of those who actively resisted.

The burnings in Coosan, ordered by Major Hervey De Montmorency, Auxiliary Intelligence officer for Westmeath, well noted for organizing large scale-arrests, was met with bitter indignation and rage among the local population. Therefore, it was decided by the IRA the actions of the Black and Tans could not go unpunished, and similar attacks should be made on the homes of local British sympathizers. This part of Westmeath was particularly rife with residences belonging to landlords with strong British ties. Other areas around south Westmeath were dotted with homes of high-ranking British military officials stationed in nearby Athlone barracks. Many had fishing and hunting lodges around Lough Ree that were unoccupied at the time, making them ideal targets. Burning the home of one of the British officials would make just as many points as any.

To make that point, the Coosan unit IRA decided to burn Moydrum Castle the home of Lord Castlemaine, a member of the British House of Lords, and Lord Lieutenant of Co. Westmeath, always an opponent of Irish National aspirations and an enemy of Ireland. He had dismissed men from his employment because they wouldn't join the British Army. The lands of Moydrum, 5,500 acres in 1680 (by the 1880s a further 11,444), along with 597 in Roscommon, were granted to the Handcock family, originally from Devon in the south west of England, during the Cromwellian plantations in the 17th century. From then on, they remained one of the most prominent landowner dynasties and landlords in the area. His wife, Lady Castlemaine and her daughter the Honourable Evelyn, along with eight servants were in continuous residence in the Castle.

Ultimately, it was Thomas 'Con' Costello the Officer Commanding the Athlone Brigade who decided on which targets, and his account explains why he opted for the Castle.

'A few days after the Tans had done their burnings, an order was received from GHQ that we were to burn an equal number of houses belonging to supporters of the British regime as a counter reprisal. There were a number of Protestants in the area, but I did not consider it would be fair to burn these people's houses for something which was not their fault. Lord Castlemaine lived in Moydrum Castle and was a member of the British House of Lords. Lady Castlemaine was in continuous residence in the Castle. I decided to burn this in preference to the small houses of other Loyalist residents, as it would be more effective. I mobilised about 20 men in all including the column. We had to go prepared to fight, as officers of the Athlone garrison were regular visitors to the Castle.'

So, Moydrum Castle was specifically selected because of its 250-years history of devout Unionism, its past of strained landlord-tenant relationships, with the delayed famine relief and the brutal response to petty crimes and evictions. However, because of the shock factor its destruction would have on the British establishment in London; to hit the spot where it would be felt most. Perhaps the targeting of one of their own, rather than some random large farmer, would hit home to the core of the British establishment.

In the early curfew hours of Sunday, 3rd July 1921 a crowd of local IRA Volunteers assembled and marched to Moydrum Castle. George would have recalled *'a party of between 30 and 40 Volunteers.'*

Whatever the exact number, it was a large group and all agreed they were heavily armed. They also carried drums of petrol, which had been procured during a previous raid on the Athlone oil depot in the Spring of 1919. Petrol, at this time, was supplied in two-gallon tins, there being no petrol pump then. With no guard of any sort on the petrol store, the Volunteers had no trouble in gaining entry.

Having removed at least a couple of hundred gallons, the tins were loaded on to a horse drawn-cart and taken to the Coosan area where they were buried in the ground. The attackers also carried several large sledgehammers with which to break down the doors if refused entry. These they got from a local forge.

Forcing their way into the darkened demesne, they dispersed for security purposes before arriving together at the castle's front door at 3.30 am. All within the castle were awakened by loud knocking.

Lady Castlemaine, getting up and looking out of her bedroom window, saw 'about sixty young men in civilian attire and carrying revolvers.' Panicking, she ordered the servants not to open the door but instead to barricade it. Costello recounts what happened next in his own words:

'Knocking at the door, we were refused admission, so we broke in one of the panels on the door with hammers which we got from a local forge. The butler and Lady Castlemaine now came to the door and asked for whoever was in charge. I told her I was in charge and told her the object of our visit. She asked me if I would allow her some time to pack some valuables and so forth, such as silverware. I pointed out to her that the Black and Tans did not give people they burned out time to even dress, but I said we did not follow their example. I gave her the time she required and also ten men to help her with the task and they took out about ten boxes of materials. Meanwhile we had

166

rounded up the staff and placed them under guard at the rear of the premises. Two armchairs were taken out of the Castle and put down for the Lady and her daughter to sit on.'

Costello's men, including George, then went about their operation. Dividing into groups they spent the next half hour going into each of the thirty-four rooms of the castle, collecting all the furniture and placing it in piles in the centre of each room. They then saturated these piles with petrol and some extra paraffin they had commandeered from the Castlemaine's chauffeur. Windows were thrown open and holes made in the floor and ceilings to give ventilation to fan the flames. Holes were made in the roof by ripping off the slates. With such a plentiful supply of air, the fire would spread rapidly, thereby ensuring maximum damage.

'The place was liberally sprinkled with petrol and then a check was made of our men to ensure that all was accounted for. I informed Lady Castlemaine that we were not criminals and were acting on the orders of GHQ of the IRA and that the burning of her home was a reprisal for the burning done by England's Black and Tans. She was very dignified under the circumstances and never winced. She thanked me for my co-operation in saving her treasures and assured me that she quite understood. The place was now alight and, having assured ourselves that it would be totally destroyed, we saluted Lady Castlemaine and withdrew. Three of our men named Costello and relatives of mine were actually working in the place. Yet, when the military interviewed Lady Castlemaine after the fire, she refused to disclose the identity of any of them and said that she was not in a position to recognize any of our party. She informed the military that the men who burned the Castle were gentlemen and behaved as such. This was told to me after by

her doctor. Lord Castlemaine was awarded £100,000 as compensation by the British Courts, which, taking into consideration the value of money then, gives an idea on the extent of the building.'

The raiders dispersed and disappeared into the darkness, leaving the Castle a raging inferno. All got away safely. As the 107-year-old, mansion went up in flames and the handful of servants raced back and forth with buckets of water to extinguish them, Lady Castlemaine and Evelyn sat huddled together on the lawn sobbing as their home disappeared before their eyes. Of the once highly-acclaimed architectural masterpiece that was Moydrum castle, only the front façade remained by daybreak. Of all the castle's contents – including priceless heirlooms, antiques, paintings, furniture and jewellery (except for some saved personal possessions and family silver plate), nothing was left. The evacuees didn't have enough time to rescue everything. By the time the police and military had arrived on the scene, the Castle and its contents were beyond salvage.

Later, at six o'clock on the evening of Sunday 3rd July, nearby Creggan House was also burnt in the same way, for the same reasons and by the same volunteers that destroyed Moydrum Castle. Creggan was seen to be just another Loyalist centre. Its occupants on the night of its burning were the servants. By eight o'clock the mansion was gutted with only the outhouses remaining.

It is fair to say that there still exists a smouldering sense of antipathy and antagonism towards the long-since disappeared Castlemaine dynasty in some areas surrounding their crumbling seat. Some still come to daub pro-Republican, anti-British messages across its historic walls. Following the establishment of the Irish Free State, much of the land belonging to the Moydrum estate was improved, divided and sold to Irish people by the Irish Land Commission.

'Six of our men in the Mountemple area were arrested by enemy forces, some of them being actually taken from their beds. It was apparent that someone in the area was supplying information to the enemy and a check was made in the area. A man named Johnston, a Protestant, who lived in the area was under suspicion for some time previously.

The officer in charge of the 2nd Battalion was in charge of this investigation. I do not know the details of what he discovered, but he was satisfied beyond doubt that Johnston was guilty. They went to Johnston's house on three or four occasions, but could never find him at home. Eventually, it was discovered that he was staying in a neighbour's house and they went there to get him. When they entered the door of the house Johnston made a dive to get away, but he was grabbed and held by our men. He fought like a lion to get free, so much so, that his coat was torn off in the struggle. It was the intention of course to take him some distance from the house and shoot him, but so violently did he fight that they were compelled to shoot him there in full view of the family in the house. The people in the house did not seem in the least surprised and it was apparent that he had told them, or they were well aware of his activities. I should have stated that in a raid on the mails, a letter was found from Johnston to the British Intelligence Authorities which seemed to indicate that he was the principal intelligence agent for the county. The O/C, 2nd Battalion will be able to give details concerning this.

After Johnston's death, the British forces carried out an extensive comb-out of the area, more intensive than even in the case of the General Lambert. They searched an area of about 40 square miles around.'

(Thomas 'Con' Costello, Witness Statement No: 1296 to the Bureau of Military History.)

Johnson's body was taken some distance from his house and having put the usual label on him *'Spies and Informers Beware'* his body was left in full view.

Following this, another spy, a man called Blagriff, a workman in the Coosan area and an ex-British soldier, was court-martialed and executed. It is understood he talked to his employer about the work he was doing for the British and when arrested, he was found with some papers belonging to him, which incriminated him.

Military courts were run by Volunteer officers. Sentences were pretty stiff if found guilty. The prisoners could be moved to other areas (*'unknown destinations'*) to safeguard the local volunteers from being identified on release – to the British. In some cases they would be deported.

Reports of the burnings in south Westmeath appeared in newspapers across Britain and Ireland. Headlines surrounding the report of the two burnings in the *Irish Times* dated 5th July 1921 reveal an Ireland in the grip of anarchy. Even with so many chaotic scenes across the country they didn't receive any local press coverage as there were no newspapers published in Athlone between October 1920 and February 1922.

The more the Troubles escalated, the more likely this scenario became, with the burnings of four big houses whose owners had gone to live on a more permanent basis in Dublin and over in England. These included the mansion of Colonel Tuite in Athlone, where a forty-man group of Volunteers razed the big house to the ground. The same squad of Volunteers burned down the house of a Captain Davin at Creggan, in Athlone, while he was in England. The dispersal of these houses in outlying areas such as south Westmeath could prove ideal strategically for the British forces in stamping out resistance. It was rumoured that the abandoned big houses were to be used as substitutes for the RIC barracks destroyed by the IRA, or worse, requisitioned as billets for the British forces. In July, the local IRA targeted and destroyed three local RIC barracks, the recently restored Brawny along with Glasson and Littleton barracks, Moyvore and Ballynacargy, and Ballymore Court House, the month having the highest number of the big house burnings so far – twenty-one in total. In the period to July 1921, County Westmeath had proven geographically to be the county with the third highest number of the big house burnings in Ireland.

With the betrayal of the tenants, the disloyalty of their servants, the destruction of their homes and the loss of their worldly possessions, the landed gentry had little reason to continue to live amidst a rapidly disintegrating and increasingly lawless and hostile society. So, they set about re-locating to England.

It would appear that Con Costello, George and the 'Boys' had a busy couple of months lighting the 'touch paper.' Burning became an excellent means of keeping the rank and file interested, and not exposing them to too many dangers or risk. It also revealed which men could be depended upon for more serious missions. To a large extent, the effectiveness of individual companies was always going to depend on the capability of a small core of individuals, like the members of the Flying Column.

CHAPTER 28

Freedom is nothing better than the chance to do better.

(Albert Camus)

Finally, on July 9th 1921, a Truce which started at noon was declared between British forces and the Irish Republican Army, the IRA agreeing to a ceasefire. The war had lasted over two and a half years and was on temporary hold. David Lloyd George, the British Prime Minister, found himself under political pressure to try and salvage something from the situation. Michael Collins later admitted the IRA, at the time of the truce, was weeks, if not days, from a collapse, with a chronic shortage of ammunition. *'Frankly, we thought they were mad,'* said Collins of the sudden offer of a Truce.

It is interesting to note that, despite the fact the newspapers heralded the upcoming Truce some days before it came into effect, and orders to the military to 'Stand Down' given just two days before, the IRA was particularly active throughout the country up to the actual day of the truce. For example, in the Westmeath area, an attack was made on the police barracks in Castlepollard.

Some days after the Truce came into effect, Eamon de Valera, as President of Sinn Fein (We Ourselves) and President (Priomh Aire) of Dail Eireann, and the Irish Republic met with British Prime Minister David Lloyd George in London four times in the week starting 14th July. He was accompanied by Austin Stack, then Chief-of-Staff IRA, and Minister for Home Affairs. Lloyd George sent de Valera his initial proposals on 20th July which were roughly in line with the Treaty that was eventually signed.

It would appear that de Valera realized the British was not prepared to offer the Irish total Independence; compromise was inevitable, a Republic was not on offer, and that any negotiation team had little or no chance to come back with a 32-counties republic. He felt that Republicans were never going to accept less, and to a man whose future self-interest was wrapped in political ambition, bringing home such an agreement could mean career suicide. He decided not to be part of the treaty delegation and maybe tainted with what more militant Republicans were bound to call a 'sell-out.' In doing so, de Valera could wait and see what Collins brought back from London and make his decision to support, or oppose, but either way he would avoid being closely identified with it.

It would seem he didn't have the courage to be party to the compromise he knew was inevitable. His bitterest opponents even accused de Valera of 'chickening out' of leading the delegation, in the knowledge the Republic could not possibly result from the negotiations in the short-term.

> *'Sean MacEoin, who proposed that Eamon de Valera became president of the Irish Republic, was to later become a severe critic of his presidential nominee. He felt that de Valera did not join the negotiating delegation for the Treaty because he was fully aware that he would achieve little more, if not less, than what Lloyd George had already offered him in London.'*

(Padraic O'Farrell, *The Sean MacEoin Story*, 1981.)

So, de Valera started to cajole Michael Collins, applying pressure on him to go as a delegate to the treaty negotiations in his place. Michael Collins was a soldier, while de Valera was a politician and leader, and as the British was old hands at getting their way in negotiations all over the world, the Irish delegation would be like babes in the wood in comparison. It was no place for a non-politician. Collins argued long and hard with de Valera, as did many others, but to no avail. Collins commented:

'...to me the task is a loathsome one. If I go, I go in the spirit of a soldier who acts against his better judgement at the orders of a superior officer.'

Collins capitulated to de Valera's wishes and negotiations started in London on the 11th October under British Prime Minster David Lloyd George, and Arthur Griffith, who headed the Irish delegation; de Valera had insisted any proposed settlement should be referred back to The Dail before being signed, which was contradicted by his bestowal of full plenipotentiary powers to his delegate team.

The men who set out with the unenviable, perhaps impossible task of trying to turn Ireland into a Republic were: Arthur Griffith, Michael Collins, Robert Barton, Eamon Duggan and George Gavin Duffy.

The English threatened immediate and terrible war within three days if the agreement on offer was rejected, and British documents have shown the threat was not made for an effect. It is believed that the British Cabinet had no scruples against a genocidal war in Ireland.

Collins believed the IRA could not sustain an all-out war with Britain and later admitted that the IRA at the time of the Truce was weeks, if not days, from a collapse with a chronic shortage of ammunition. Certainly, Collins would have been one of the finest judges of this. The idea he might be responsible for a renewal of war was too much for him. With just two hours to decide, and believing the British proposals were the best deal they were going to get, he exercised his plenipotentiary rights and agreed to sign.

The deed was done at 14.30 hours on the 6th December 1921 eventually leading to the establishment of the Irish Free State.

Winston Churchill said of Collins, '*In all my life, I have never seen so much passion and suffering in restraint.*'

After he had signed, Lord Birkenhead, the British Lord Chancellor who had befriended Collins during the Treaty negotiations, said to him, '*I have signed my political death-warrant*' – to which Collins replied:

> '*I may have signed my actual death-warrant. I want to say that there was never an Irishman placed in such a position as I was by reason of these negotiations.*'
> (Michael Collins.)

Some hours after signing the Treaty Collins wrote:

> '*I tell you this, early this morning I signed my death warrant. I thought at the time, how odd, how ridiculous – a bullet may just as well have done the job five years ago. Think – what have I got for Ireland? Something which she has wanted these past seven hundred years. Will anyone be satisfied at the bargain? Will anyone?*'
> (Michael Collins.)

> '*Through its repeated failure by 1920 to deliver Home Rule in a form acceptable to the great majority of the population of Ireland, the British Government forfeited the right that it had*

assumed for itself in the act of the Union to play the role of arbiter of Ireland's destiny. Lloyd George recognized as much the following year when he finally agreed to enter formally, into negotiations with representatives of Sinn Fein which had emerged as a legitimate, rival arbiter of Irish Affairs. The political solution finally agreed on by signatories to the Anglo-Irish Treaty of December 1921 was a modification of the provisions of the Government of Ireland Act (1920), which provided for two political entities – an Ulster Unionist dominated Northern Ireland of 6 counties, remaining as an integral part of the United Kingdom, and a nationalist dominated Irish Free State of 26 counties, with the status of a dominion of the British Empire. None of the parties to this agreement was really satisfied, all had to compromise, and the outcome they were striving to achieve – peace and stability in the island of Ireland has remained elusive.'

(John Ainsworth, School of Humanities & Social Science, Queensland University of Technology.)

'It is not fear of losing more lives that compelled a reluctant offer from England but it is the shame of any further imposition of agony upon a people that loves liberty above everything else.'

(Mahatma Ghandi, said of the British peace offer.)

It was felt by the pro-Treaty faction, the Treaty was the best opportunity for Irish men and women to rule their own country, and in the fullness of time bring the disputed six counties back into a fully united Ireland. Michael Collins argued that it gave *'not the ultimate freedom that all nations aspire and develop, but freedom to achieve freedom.'*

As time would tell, it was the best deal on offer for the Irish. In

1922, Britain could never grant Ireland an independent Republic, without similar demands being made from Dominions like Australia, Canada and New Zealand.

On 7th January 1922, in the vote that followed, Dail Eireann (the parliament of the Republic) narrowly passed the Anglo-Irish Treaty by 64 votes to 57, so ending the War of Independence. In voting for the presidency of the Dail on 10th January 1922, Eamon de Valera was defeated by sixty votes to fifty eight. He left the Dail accompanied by his followers.

Following this, a new 'Provisional Government' (Rialtas Sealadach na hEireann), headed by Michael Collins and Arthur Griffiths, was set up to transfer power from the British Administration for the Irish Free State.

Not so, de Valera, now the leader of the Anti-Treaty lobby, at a speech in Dundalk, again denied the legitimacy of the provisional government and ridiculed the London agreement. His own proposals published in January 1922 fell far short of an autonomous all-Ireland republic. However, the general election on 18th June 1922 gave overwhelming support for the Pro-Treaty party. Both parties went into the Irish general election as hostile, both calling themselves Sinn Fein. The Pro-Treaty won the election by 239,193 votes to 133,864 for Anti-Treaty. A further 237,226 people voted for other parties, most of whom supported the Treaty. The election showed the majority of the Irish Electorate supported the Treaty and the foundation of the Irish Fee State; de Valera is quoted as saying, *'The majority have no right to do wrong.'*

For George, who took part in most of the major conflicts in Athlone, the County of Westmeath and south Roscommon and continuing his Volunteer duties, managed to avoid capture by the Crown forces until the Truce of July 11 and for his Commander-in-Chief Michael Collins, the Treaty was to have tragic consequences. With the Truce in place, George returned to his home in Moate to take part, once again, in family life with the hope the killing and violence were over for good. He started to see a young lady in Clara and joined a drama group in Athlone taking a role in their 1922 production. This touring group is believed to have been used to move weapons and ammunition around the county during 'The Troubles.'[6]

[6] The total number of IRA Volunteers killed in the guerrilla war of 1919-1921 is given as 550 (including 24 official executions) and about 200 civilians. RIC / Black and Tan deaths 418, British army deaths 261.

CHAPTER 29

THE IRISH CIVIL WAR

28th June 1922 - 24th May 1923

Between the Pro-Treaty Irish Free State Army and the anti-Treaty IRA

All wars are civil wars because all men are brothers
(François Fenelon)

In the six months leading up to the outbreak of civil war, Collins tried desperately to heal the rift in the nationalist movement.

'If the price of peace is the blacking of my name, then it's the price I'll gladly pay.'

(Michael Collins.)

The conflict that followed was waged between the forces of the Irish Free State, who supported the Anglo-Irish Treaty and the Republican opposition for whom the Treaty represented a betrayal of the Republic with regard to the status of the six counties in Northern Ireland remaining under British rule. During the Civil War, the Anti-Treaty factions were led nominally by Eamon de Valera, who had resigned as President of the Republic on the treaty's ratification, giving his support to the dissident IRA members who took up arms against the Treaty.

The Irish Provisional Government established the Irish Free State on 6th December 1922, and set about organising the National

Army in place of the IRA. It was envisaged that the new army would be built around the disbanded Pro-Treaty IRA. Its size was estimated at 7,000 men.

Comdt. George Adamson, Captain Sean Rattigan, Captain Patrick Rattigan

George joined the new National Army in January 1922, his army number being O.3516. His commanding officer was Commandant General Sean MacEoin who, along with the rest of his County Longford command, also sided with the Pro-Treaty forces. George was joined in the Army by his brothers, Commandant Joseph (Josey) P. Adamson and William Adamson from Moate, and Sergeant John (Johnny) Adamson, of Clara, all ex-IRA. The Provisional Government of the Irish Free State set up five command areas, one of which was the Midland Division under General Sean MacEoin, with its headquarters in Athlone barracks.

General Sean MacEoin and Brigade Staff Officers The Castle Athlone Feb 1922
General MacEoin second from left front row.
Comdt. George Adamson second from left back row.
Photograph courtesy Irish Army, Custume Barracks, Athlone.

On Monday 28th February 1922 George, as a senior officer in the Division, and wearing peak cap, a uniform of smooth green serge, a tunic with patch pockets and rank-markings, green whipcord riding breeches with polished leggings, leather straps, pouches and holster, proudly marching at the head of his troops, was prominent in the take-over from the British Forces of Victoria Barracks, which was promptly renamed Custume Barracks.

With a detachment of the Athlone Brigade in the van, Comdt. George Adamson, on left, and Vice Comdt. Kit McKeown lead troops of the Irish Army into Custume Barracks, on February 28, 1922, on take-over from the British.

He then joined his Commanding Officer Commandant General Sean MacEoin, in the take-over and raising of the Tricolour on Athlone Castle, accompanied by Comdt. Tony Lawler, Comdt. Ned Cooney Comdt. Barry McGiffe and Capt. Con Costello.

'In Athlone this Tuesday was seen one of the most striking results of the Treaty – the military barracks, so long a buttress of English power in the Midlands and west was formally vacated by British troops and handed over to the Irish Republican Army, headed with perfect discipline took possession.

> *The next and perhaps the most moving scene of the day was the hoisting of the tricolour on the Castle, which was not without its touch of humour. When Gen. MacEoin and his staff arrived to unfurl the flag, it was discovered that there was no flag-staff. However, G.V. Simmons, the local photographer, contributed in his way to the historic occasion by presenting the mast of his yacht as a flag-staff.'* (Westmeath Independent).

In the lead-up to the outbreak of the Civil War, pro-Treaty and anti-Treaty supporters were forced to choose sides. Supporters of the Treaty came to be known as 'Free State Army' although they were legally the 'National Army' and were often called 'Staters' by their opponents. The latter called themselves 'Republicans' and were also known as 'Irregulars'. Each Volunteer now had to choose a side in the fight that was to follow, and it was not unknown for a Volunteer to switch sides, in joining the Free State Army, and having been issued with a rifle and equipment, doing a 'runner' to the opposite side taking his newly issued kit with him.

The split over the Treaty was deeply personal. Many of the leaders on both sides had been close friends and comrades during the War of Independence. This made their lethal disagreement over the Treaty more bitter. In some families the Civil War set brother against brother and comrades in arms became sworn enemies. This generated a deep hatred that would last for years to come.

During this period Dublin was buzzing with rumours of a possible attempt by the Republicans to rush the Dail Eireann and purge it, like Charles I's, Long Parliament, by military force. The Dublin Chamber of Commerce, a body of mixed politics, held a well-attended meeting at which deep concern was expressed for the present lack of security to life and property. There was condemnation voiced against those who *'are playing freakishly with the vulnerable machines of trade'*.

Sir Horace Plunkett, the chief speaker, said he thought the people of the United States must be puzzled to know what was happening in Ireland at the time. He supported the Provisional Government because it was doing its best to obtain freedom for Ireland, showing high courage in this effort. The British Government was not responsible for the trouble. It was the Irish themselves. Sir Horace added, the present policy of some of the young men seemed to be to transfer the authority from the orb and sceptre, to the bayonet and the bomb.

CHAPTER 30

The real tragedy of civil war brings the agony of fighting family and former friends on the other side. In this the Irish Civil War was no exception.

(Albert Camus)

Before this, the start of the war, there were a number of armed confrontations between the opposing IRA factions. In February, an Anti-Treaty IRA unit under Ernie O'Malley seized the RIC barracks in Clonmel taking forty policemen prisoner and capturing 600 rifles and thousands of rounds of ammunition. In March, a force of 800 Anti-Treaty fighters under O'Malley attempted to take over the military barracks in Limerick. More confrontations resulted in the occupation of the former British garrisons at Birr, Renmore and Templemore. Again in March, Anti-Treaty units in Cork raided a British Warship, the *HMS Upnor,* and captured up to 1,500 rifles, 50 handguns and over 25,000 rounds of ammunition, which they then distributed to other anti-Treaty units.

During a speaking tour of Ireland beginning on St. Patrick's Day, 17th March 1922, de Valera, in controversial anti-treaty speeches at Carrick on Suir, Lismore, Dungarvan and Waterford, set the ground rules, and tone for the horrors that were to follow, when he said:

> 'If the Treaty were accepted, the fight for freedom would still go on, and the Irish people, instead of fighting foreign soldiers, will have to fight Irish soldiers of an Irish government.'

In a speech at Thurles, several days later, he added that the (Anti-Treaty) IRA

> '...would have to wade through the blood of the soldiers of the Irish Government, and perhaps through that of some members of the Irish Government to get their freedom.'

In a letter to the *Irish Independent* on 23rd March 1922 he accepted the accuracy of their report of his comment *'wading through the blood'*, but deplored the fact that the newspaper had published it.

On 26th March, Anti-Treaty Leaders held an 'Army Convention' in the Mansion House in Dublin, which was attended by de Valera, where they voted to repudiate the Treaty. They also rejected the authority of the Dail to accept the Treaty and set up their own sixteen-man 'Army Executive', all anti-Treaty members of the IRA, led by Liam Lynch, Liam Mellows and Rory O'Connor. The new Executive announced the authority of the Minister of Defence, and the Chief of Staff of the National Army would no longer be accepted. This situation posed a considerable threat as Anti-Treaty commanders and their troops occupied certain barracks belonging to the new state.

Shortly after the Army Convention in March, Paddy Morrissey, Athlone, the local IRA Brigade Commander, who served as an Anti-Treaty delegate to the outlawed Convention, approached Colonel Commandant Tony Lawler, O/C Custume Barracks, in the absence of Sean MacEoin, and told him he and his men were taking the Anti-Treaty side. On the return of C/O Sean MacEoin, he spoke to Morrissey, who stated that he, his officers and men would not obey any orders from the government.

During the disagreement in what was *ipso facto* a mutiny,

MacEoin stripped Morrissey of his Sam Brown belt and expelled him, along with his Anti-Treaty officers and men from the barracks – a humiliation not soon forgotten. The Republicans did not move far away but set up their headquarters in the nearby Claxton's Royal Hotel.

Following the confrontation between the two senior officers, George, who had done so much to train the Athlone Brigade during the Tan War and served for two and a half years in the Athlone Flying Squad, was promoted to Brigadier General in place of Morrissey.

The Midland Division, in the main Pro-Treaty, now covered the Counties of Longford, Westmeath, the middle of County Cavan and the east of Counties Fermanagh and Leitrim.

Brigadier General George Adamson

Brig. Gen. George Adamson standing beside an artillery piece in Custume Barracks, Athlone, Co. Westmeath, 1922.Photograph courtesy Irish Army, Custume Barracks. Athlone.

On 2nd April, the Anti-Treaty faction of the Irish Republican Army held a large parade in Dublin; de Valera took the salute at a March past of Anti-Treaty forces in County Clare. It soon became clear they were endeavouring to prevent the Irish Free State from coming into existence and speeches were made by persons who claimed to represent the majority of the Irish Republican Army. In County Mayo, Michael Collins was prevented from speaking to the people.

Then, on 24th April 1922, just eight weeks after taking over the Castle and barracks on 28th February, and assuming the mantle of Brigadier General in command of the 1st Midlands Brigade, George was shot once again.

On the night of 24th, George returned late to the barracks following a visit to his parents in Moate. After midnight, and for certain military reasons, he led a party of officers who included Capt. Patrick Fitzpatrick, to take in a suspicious motor car parked in the street outside the Royal Hotel. They succeeded in getting the car, but on arrival at the barracks, they discovered one of the officers was missing.

So, at two o'clock on a mild and misty Monday morning of 25th April 1922, George, with courage characteristic of him, left the barracks to search for him. He was accompanied by his close friend Captain Sean Rattigan, Captain Walsh, a Lt. Liam O'Meara, and one other officer. Before they got to Irishtown Captain Rattigan broke off and went elsewhere. Arriving in Irishtown, they challenged a man standing in a doorway near Avondale House. They ordered him to put his hands up, but he did not comply. One of the officers covered him with his revolver. The man spoke to George: *'I know you George and you know me.'* The man then asked about the car that was taken. However, before the conversation could continue, the group were surrounded by nine armed men who called out, *'Hands up!'*

Surrounded, George and his officers had no alternative but to comply. The order was obeyed and the accompanying officers were taken aside and disarmed. Then, still holding his hands up in response to the challenge and while looking away from the man in the doorway towards the new arrivals, the man levelled a revolver at George and fired point blank into the back of his head. The bullet tore through his skull exiting from his left ear, knocking him to the ground mortally wounded. He had been struck once again by the clenched fist of fate. He was carried into nearby Avondale House which was quite close to the scene of the tragedy and messengers sent for a doctor and priest.

Rev Father J.J. Goodwin was first to arrive followed by Father Columba, O.F.M. A few moments after, Dr Thomas McDonnell, King Street, Athlone arrived, having been alerted by a messenger that George had been shot and had been moved to Avondale House. He arrived at the scene soon after 2 p.m. to find George in an unconscious condition. Father Goodwin administered the last sacraments as a Dr Chapman arrived.

Both doctors noticed George had a wound in his left ear which was bleeding freely. With the help of Dr Chapman, Dr McDonnell plugged the wound and both doctors did everything they could to revive the wounded George. He became semi-conscious but was unable to answer questions. He asked to be taken home to bed as he was feeling very tired. The doctors, having bandaged his head, moved him to the Military Hospital in Custume Barracks. There, he was also attended by Dr Cooney the military doctor, but to no avail. George passed away at 10 o'clock on Tuesday morning.

By a sad and strange coincidence, he died on the day of his 25th birthday on the 25th April. It was said at the time that the bullet, fired by a fellow Irishman, was the first shot in the Civil War of the unhappy period.

It would appear George had a premonition he was about to die. On the day before the shooting, he escorted General Sean MacEoin to Duffy's where he was to be billeted overnight. When he was leaving, George pointed to a ring he was wearing; he took it off and shoved it on MacEoin's finger and said, *'Every time you look at that, think of me.'*

At 6 o'clock in the morning, the town was surrounded by troops under Sean MacEoin. He issued an ultimatum to the commandant of the irregular troops, charging him, his officers and men with conspiring to murder George, charged them with murder and called on them to surrender.

He allowed them fifteen minutes for a reply, at the expiration of which time he would open fire as the lawful authority charged with peace in the district. Commandant Francis 'Frank' Fitzpatrick, in command of the Irregulars, replied he had no choice but to surrender. He assured MacEoin that he was in no way responsible for the deed, which he sincerely regretted. The surrendered officers and men were brought to the barracks of the regular troops and detained.

CHAPTER 31

Woe to the hand that shed this costly blood.
(William Shakespeare))

The tricolour on the castle and barracks was lowered immediately, which was the first intimation the townspeople got of the sad news. In a short time, crowds were collecting around the gate; women sobbed and soldiers cried, realising the great loss of their beloved Brigadier. The scenes were affecting in the extreme. At noon, the remains were laid out in state at the morgue in the Military Hospital, and a guard of honour placed around the bier. Immediately, the barrack gates were thrown open to the public, and there were touching scenes of people visiting the military barracks to pay homage to their dead hero. Throughout the day, there were continuous queues of people, men, women and children, who knelt beside the bier in turn and prayed for the happy repose of his soul. In all, it is estimated that 5,000 people passed through the morgue that Tuesday. It appeared that the whole town was in mourning for George who was extremely popular.

His father, mother, brothers and sisters were pathetic figures beside the bier for the greater portion of the day and the sympathy of the public and the army went out to them in the loss of their dear and affectionate son and brother. All the local clergy and leading citizens called on General Sean MacEoin and Colonel-Commandant Lawlor and personally rendered their sympathy, and of the people of Athlone.

Brig. Gen. George Adamson 1897 – 1922 (25 years) Killed outside Avondale Irishtown
Mon 25 Apr 1922 and laid out in Custume Barracks Tue 26 Apr 1922 [7]
Photograph courtesy Irish Army, Custume Barracks, Athlone.

In the afternoon, his Lordship the Most Rev Dr Hoare, Bishop of Ardagh, and Clonmacnoise with the Very Rev Canon Langan D.D., Parish Priest Moate, entered Custume Barracks and tendered their sympathy to the General.

Bishop Hoare, at a Confirmation Ceremony at St. Mary's church that Tuesday morning, referring to the tragedy, said that the parish stood astounded at the act committed the previous night:

> '*May God forgive the murderer,*' he said; '*He will be an unhappy man all the days of his life. Cain, where is your brother? Where is your brother's blood? He cries to Heaven for vengeance. It is a shocking thing to see these things happening, but they will happen as long as we have two contending armies, one against another, and as long as we have every young man*

---

[7] Spot the ghostly apparition in the photograph.

having a pistol in his pocket. You cannot expect civilization and you cannot expect unity among the people as long as that goes on. After 700 years we have a Government of our own, the de jure and de facto Government. It is our duty to give that Government our loyalty and fealty. There should be one army and not two. Pray hard that God may save us, and our country, from revolution for years and years. Pray that God may have mercy on the poor man that was shot, and pray God may have mercy on the murderer of that unfortunate man.'

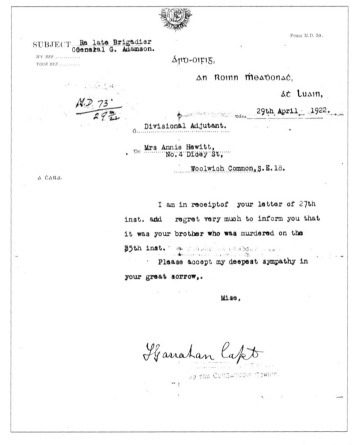

Copy of original letter sent to George's sister Mrs Annie Hewitt (nee Adamson), then residing in London, informing her of the murder of her brother.

CHAPTER THIRTY ONE

*The funeral procession crossing over the Bridge of Athlone with the Castle
and Barracks in the background.
Photograph courtesy Irish Army, Custume Barracks, Athlone.*

The funeral, attended by dignitaries of church and state and a
large concourse of people, took place on the 28th April 1922 in
Mount Temple old churchyard, where he was laid to rest with full
military honours, beside the Tormey brothers.

> 'I had not expected anything but death to end my part in
> the struggle; we had seen the grey face of death too often
> not to be able to know his shadow as we wandered. We did
> not expect to live through the war; there were too many
> risks to be taken, but we did feel that our cause would win.
> (Ernie O'Malley, On Another Man's Wound: A
> Personal History of Ireland's War of Independence.)

An tOglach, the Army paper of the time, dated the 25th April 1922, published the following report:

'IRISH OFFICER MURDERED
Distinguished Soldier's Tragic End

'In the death of Brigadier-General Adamson, O.C. Athlone Brigade, the Irish Army loses one of its most chivalrous and distinguished officers. On Monday night, midnight, Brigadier Adamson was held up by an armed party in the streets of Athlone, and called upon to put his hands up. He complied with the order, and was then done to death in a most cowardly and callous act. A revolver was placed against his head and discharged. He fell mortally wounded, and died ten hours later. The late Brigadier Adamson earned a high record for valour during the late war in Ireland. He also took part in the European war, and was awarded the D.C.M. of the British Army for conspicuous gallantry on the field. The crime caused a sensation in Athlone, where the deceased officer had earned general esteem and respect.'

The newspaper reported that in the Army, his loss is irreplaceable. It goes on to say:

> *'He was a gallant officer, idolised by brother officers and men. His army record both in the Irish and British Armies was most brilliant.'*

On 10th October 1922, the Catholic Bishops of Ireland issued a formal statement, describing the anti-Treaty campaign as

> *'...a system of murder and assassination of National forces without any legitimate authority...the guerrilla warfare now*

being carried on [by] the Irregulars is without moral sanction and therefore the killing of National soldiers is murder before God, the seizing of public and private property, the breaking of roads and bridges and railways is criminal. All who in contravention of this teaching, participate in such crimes are guilty of grievous sins and may not be absolved in Confession nor admitted to Holy Communion if they persist in such evil courses.'

CHAPTER THIRTY ONE

WHO KILLED
GEORGE ADAMSON and WHY?

The first casualty when war comes is truth
(Hiram Johnson)

As far as can be seen it would appear that an Anti-Treaty IRA man had heeded de Valera's clarion call by *'wading through the blood of'* 25 years-old George. His shooting produced many conspiracy theories among the people of Moate and Athlone in particular, as to the identity and motives of his assassin and from within his family, who still believe his assassination was ordered by some of the officer corps of the National Army. George's murder is a mystery. If you, the reader, can add to the evidence, or give a rational explanation for the lack of it, in some way help to unravel or solve this eighty-year-old 'Cold Case', or if you know the names of the other officers who accompanied George on that fateful foray, or the names of the Anti-Treaty men at the scene, I would be most grateful if you could please correspond with me through my publishers.

Go raibh maith agat
(Thank You)

EPILOGUE

"Honourable age does not depend on length of days,
nor is the number of years a true measure of life.'

(The Book of Wisdom)

'We need heroes. We have always needed heroes. It is part of the human condition to yearn towards selfless nobility, to idolise the men and women who can make of us, more than the stick figures surrounding the animals in the cave-drawings in Lascaux. Without the possibility of heroism, we stand as pathetic as those tiny human representations, overwhelmed by the terrible random malignant power of the world around us. The hero confirms the glad possibility, that we each carry within us the seeds of becoming more than we are.'

(Terry Prone, 'Saturday Essay', *Irish Daily Mail*.)

No doubt that George was such a hero, a great man and a great soldier. His young life was a pattern of true heroism, as repeatedly he found himself in deadly situations. His courage saw him through physical pain and discomfort, with hardship and great danger added for good measure. He stood up for his beliefs, no matter what the cost. He appears to have had phenomenal levels of emotional commitment and motivation, and tremendous courage in taking on a system hell-bent on his destruction. He faced down fear, finally becoming a martyr for something more important than himself. He lived his life with dignity and high dedication, and there is little doubt that he had a strong spiritual belief to pull him through tough times, that inner strength that never dies.

> 'The true revolutionary is guided by strong feelings of love. It is impossible to think of an authentic revolutionary without this quality... One must have a large dose of humanity, a large dose of sense of justice and truth, to avoid falling into extremes, into cold intellectualism, into isolation from the masses. Every day we must struggle so that this love of living humanity is transformed into concrete facts, into acts that will serve as an example.'

(Ernesto de la Serna 'Che' Guevara, *Socialism and the man in Cuba* (1965).)

A life cut short with no later years, George never lived to see the future of his sacrifice and lost youth. All he had to contribute to Ireland was now gone. A great Irishman and patriot, he lies buried in an unmarked grave under a wilderness of weeds, overgrown brambles and nettles, impenetrable, in the disused and unattended graveyard of Dunegan Holy Trinity Cemetery, Mount Temple, Moate, Co. Westmeath, Eire.in such sad and sorry circumstances, with the other dead heroes of the Moate Fianna.[8] Sadly, it appears, there is nobody to cherish this noble burial ground.[9] But at least, George is in the company of his friends and fellow warriors. The Irish Republic of today bears witness that their suffering was not meaningless or devoid of grace.

---

[8] The Fianna were a band of Irish warriors of the 2nd and 3rd centuries which formed a military elite that guarded the high king of Ireland.

[9] Perhaps the voluntary workers of the National Graves Association, formed in 1926, may wish to look into the state of the graves of George, Jim and Joe as it is their raison d'être to remember and honour the deeds of those who died for Ireland.

'*Stranger pause and shed a tear - a nation's heart lies buried here.*'
(Lincolnshire Yeomanry)

Footnote: In Celtic mythology *Tir Na Og* (Land of Eternal Youth), is an Otherworld realm, where sickness and death do not exist, a place of eternal youth and beauty. Where, music, strength, life and all pleasurable pursuits come together in one place. Do we not hope George and his brothers in arms inhabit this land in the peace they lived and died for?

ROLL OF HONOUR

'Life springs from death; and the from the graves of patriot men and women spring living nations.'
(Patrick Pearse)

IN COMMEMORATION

To those members of the

**THE IRISH REPUBLICAN ARMY ATHLONE BRIGADE
1916 – 1922**

who gave their lives in actions against,

BRITISH CROWN FORCES

KILLED IN ACTION, DIED OF WOUNDS

'THE BEST AND THE BRAVEST

GEORGE ADAMSON
MICHAEL BANNON
DICK BIRTLES
JOHN BLANEY
SEAN CALVIN

JOHN CARTY

SEAN COSTELLO

JOE CUNNINGHAM

SEAMUS FINN

BERNARD 'BRIAN' GAFFEY

MICHAEL GAFFEY

THOMAS HUGHES

GEORGE MANNING

TOM 'TOBY' MANNION

BERNARD McCORMACK

CHRISTOPER 'KIT' McKEOWN

JOE MORRISSEY

PATRICK SEERY

PATRICK SLOAN

JAMES 'JIM' TORMEY

JOSEPH TORMEY

'Freedom isn't Free … someone had to pay for it'

APPENDIX

When the story of these times gets written, we want it to say we did all
we could, and it was more than anyone could have imagine.
(Bono)

The sacrifices that these men made in 1919-1922 are every bit as
relevant now as they were then. Possibly even more so, in a world
where most people have no concept of selflessness and comradeship.
Sadly, those in a position to cause a change have abysmally failed
to recognise this. The disgraceful state of the Dunegan Holy Trinity
Cemetery, Mount Temple, Moate, Co. Westmeath, Eire is a case
in point.

On 21st January 1941, the Irish Government announced the
creation of a medal, the 'Cagadh na Saoirse' (meaning the Fight
for Freedom), awarded to IRA Volunteers who took part in the War
of Independence. It bears a ribbon with two vertical stripes, half
black and half tan, the colour symbolic of the Black and Tans. In
the centre is a figure purported to be typical of the Irish Flying
Column of the period. It is erect and facing the front, wearing a
trench coat and cap, leggings, boots, a Sam Brown belt, and a
bandolier, a holstered pistol against its right side, with a slung rifle
at its left. Across the middle of the medal is the word 'EIRE'.

This medal and ribbon was issued to those who were not deemed
to have been on active service during the War, but who were
members of the old-Irish Republican Army. Whereas men with
actual active and armed service, such as the famous 'Flying
Columns, were awarded the medal adorned with the
'Comrac' (meaning combat) bar.

Unfortunately, for George's memory, the Irish Government and Military appear to have deemed he was not eligible for the medal as his family were never issued with one. In 1944 his widowed mother wrote the following letter:

'Secretary, Military Service Medals Award Branch,
Colaiste Caoimhn,
Glasnevin.

Dear Sir,

I have the honour of making application for Military Service Medal, on behalf of my son the late Brigadier General George Adamson, Moate, Co. Westmeath. General McKeown T.D. & Col. T. Lawler can verify.

Trusting to hear from you earliest.
Yours faithfully.
Elizabeth Adamson.'

It took the Military Service Medals Branch four years for the application to be investigated and reply sent to his mother. Following this a Service Medal without Bar was issued. Posthumously awarded medals were numbered and Medal No 524 was awarded in respect of George. It would appear that the Irish Government and the Military authorities did not recognize George's active service, which started about June 1919 and his service in the Athlone Flying Column from its inception in October 1920 to the Truce on 9th July 1921, as entitlement for the award of the Medal with Comrac Bar.

The following, a letter to the editor of a local paper shows the annoyance and frustration of a family member with this situation:

'Dear Editor,

Now I wonder if you can help me with a small problem.

I have sent emails to President Mary MacAleese, Minister of State Conor Lenihan, Deputy Mary O'Rourke, Eddie Fitzgerald at the Department of Defence and An Taoiseach Bertie Ahern. I have been trying for over 10 years to get this resolved.

In a nutshell I am trying to put right a wrong done to my family, in particular my late uncle George Adamson of Moate who was killed in an ambush in 1922.

He should have been awarded the Service Medal Class A Combat medal with bar for his active service in the War of Independence which was well recorded. Instead he was granted posthumously the lesser Service medal without bar for non-combatants. He was involved in two ambushes with British forces, was shot in the lungs in one of them, and Deputy Commandant for the Athlone Brigade. How much combat did he need?

I seem to be hitting bureaucracy gone a wee bit naff. I am told that it was too long ago by the Department of Defence. The President can't interfere with Government departments, and so on. I haven't heard anything from Mary O'Rourke so I wrote again yesterday. Conor Lenihan, TD, really tried to help.

I get the impression from the Department of Defence quite frankly that they can't be bothered and they think I am some sort of crank. If it is cranky to honour a genuine hero of the Republic and rectify a wrong and see the decent thing done, then I guess I am cranky, but not ashamed of it. All it takes is

*a look at the evidence and amend the award. As it seems the
great and the good can't do it, do you think the press could help?
I live in Scotland but my family the Adamsons are still in Moate
and Horseleap. The castle have eventually put a bit of a notice
up in the grounds but the literature makes no mention of the
change of name... to Adamson Castle in honour of uncle
George. I am getting on in years now and I don't think anyone
else will pick up the gauntlet for me*

Slan Go Foill
Yours etc.
Liam Hackett.'

The comment by Liam Hackett about Athlone Castle is an
interesting and sad one. In September 1968, for a brief period, the
once royal castle of Athlone was renamed Adamson
Castle/Caislean Mhic Adam in honour of Brig. Gen. Adamson and
the Athlone Brigade. However, it was felt, by some, that such a re-
naming was most inappropriate. This appears to ignore the fact that
from 1691 to 11th July 1921, for the greater part of three centuries,
it was the buttress of English military power in the midland and
the west, the seat and centre of oppressive action. That, as Athlone
Castle, it is a national monument to, and a concrete symbol of,
seven hundred years of tyrannical, imperial rule. In 1922 Victoria
Barracks, Athlone, was re-named Custume Barracks to honour the
heroic Sergeant Custume, a non-commissioned officer of Dragoons,
who earned everlasting glory during the 1691 Siege when he lead
volunteers out under Dutch guns to tear down the planks of the
hastily constructed wooden Bridge of Athlone in the face of an
invading army. Their heroism and sacrifice inspired others of the

Irish Army to die in completing the task. For that action Sgt. Custume was accorded the following accolade from General Charles de Claremont, Marquis de St. Ruth for – *'no braver deed was ever done before in history.'*

The men who died bravely with Sgt. Custume were not named, but are implicitly honoured by both General St Ruth, and in the re-naming of the barracks and a street in Athlone.

Therefore, in the matter of the re-naming of Athlone Castle to Adamson Castle, is it not implicit that the men of the Athlone Brigade are also honoured?

Sgt. Custume and his fellow soldiers were rightly honoured for their single action on the bridge against great odds. Is it not right then, to honour Brig. Gen. Adamson and the men of the Athlone Brigade, IRA, who over a two and a half year period, enacted many acts of bravery and in some cases gave their lives in the fight for an Independent Ireland?

In reporting the re-naming ceremony a local paper made the following quote:

> *'In unveiling the plaque to the memory of Adamson, Gen. MacEoin included the names of all those whose records were similar in the period 1920/22.'*

Is it not time to publicly re-affirm the renaming of Athlone Castle to Adamson Castle/Caislean Mhic Adam and give honour where honour is due?

It is interesting to note that on the 28th January 1971, Dail Eireann in Oral Answers, Volume 251 – Flying of the National Flag, the following question was put:

Question: 73. Mr Cooney asked the Minister for Finance if he will arrange to continue to have the national flag flown over Adamson Castle, Athlone.

Mr Cooney: *'In view of the fact that this castle was a symbol of foreign domination for over 700 years and during that time a foreign flag flew over it, would the minister not agree that it would be symbolic and quite proper if the national flag would fly over it as it has flown over it ever since we got our freedom in 1921?'*

It is also interesting to note that for visitors to Ireland, the Collins Touring Map of Ireland 1998 is helpful in indicating Adamson Castle in red, block capitals.

If anything was learned from the Irish Fight for Independence, it showed that the outcome was not determined by the number of combatants on both sides. In essence, size doesn't guarantee success (the David and Goliath story) and that in a guerrilla war if you don't lose, you win. A situation which is borne out by the effect and influence on the future of Ireland then and now. Many military historians have concluded that the IRA fought a largely successful and lethal guerrilla war, which forced the British government to believe that the IRA could not be defeated militarily. The Black and Tans were never able to cope with men like George and the 'Boys' of the Athlone Brigade, who used classic guerrilla tactics against them.

George's brother Joseph (Josey) P. Adamson became Acting-Brigadier on George's death, he had been an active member of the Athlone Brigade. His work as a linesman enabled him to tap into the lines from British Army H.Q. and RIC H.Q. in Dublin and intercept their messages to British Midlands and Western

Commands. He was also employed by the Brigade in cutting railway, telegraph and telephone lines/wires, when necessary.

L to R: Joe (Josey) Adamson (Vice Brig. Gen. having taken over his murdered brothers position and rank) - Pat Naughton - Mick Calumn - Sean O'Farrell - Tom Moore - Jimmy Duffy - Tommy Dully.

Josey was in charge of a party of Free State soldiers when one of his men John Blaney, from Gairnafailish, Athlone, was shot and killed in an ambush by Anti-Treaty men. Blaney had been a stalwart in the IRA and served as a Company Captain of the Berries Company, 3rd Battalion Athlone Brigade, and also associated with the Coosan Company in Co. Westmeath. His Brother-in-Law Jimmy Mannion of the 1st Battalion and one of the first Free State Army soldiers to enter Athlone barrack with George and Sean MacEoin on the take-over from the British.

Some time after that action Josey resigned his commission in the army, it is believed, to follow the man who murdered his brother George to America to exact revenge. He never returned, choosing to settle in New Jersey, Jersey City, USA, where he married and raised a family. A kind and generous man, he regularly sent money home for many years, to help to support his family in Ireland.

The Civil War, though short, was bloody, cost the lives of not only George and his friend and comrade Christopher 'Kit' McKeown, who joined the Anti-Treaty forces and was shot dead in Moate on Sunday morning 13th November 1922, but many public figures, including Michael Collins himself.

Dick Birtles from Drumraney, O/C 2nd Battalion, a member of the Flying Column and O/C of the successful ambush at Auburn, was killed in Low Street during the Civil War, having been sheltered for the night by Miss Hogan and Miss Kavanagh in the teacher's residence. He called to Cunningham's the following morning where he was shot. The Parish Priest of Ballymore, Fr. Casey, made the following entry in the parish death register:

Richard Birtles. Shot in the back by Riggs, an ex-British Army private, in Nicholas Cunningham's yard by Free State soldiers.

Collins had travelled to his home county to contact Anti-Treaty leaders, and propose a Truce and bring the Civil War to an end. However, on 22nd August 1922, his party was ambushed by Anti-Treaty forces near the village of Beal na mBlaith (The Mouth of Flowers). During the twenty-minute gun battle that followed Michael Collins was shot dead. His body, brought back to Dublin, lay in state for three days in Dublin City Hall, where tens of thousands of mourners filed past his coffin to pay their last respects. The funeral took place in Dublin's Pro Cathedral, where a number of foreign dignitaries were in attendance. His burial took place in Glasnevin Cemetery, Dublin.

Among his many achievements in his short but eventful life, he was appointed Minister of Finance in the new government and, as stated earlier, immediately set about floating a loan for some millions of pounds. He was so successful in this venture that, following the October Revolution, the new Russian Republic sought a loan of $25,000 from the Irish Republic using the Russian Crown Jewels as collateral.

They were handed over to Harry Boland in New York and were kept in his mother's house during the War of Independence, and given over to the Irish Government in 1938. They were placed in a safe, in a Government building, and forgotten about. Following their discovery in 1948 they were eventually returned to the Soviet Union in 1950 in return for the original $ 25,000.

Eamon de Valera, who strongly supported the Anti-Treaty side during the Civil War, reconsidered his views while in jail and came to accept the idea of political activity under the terms of the Free State constitution. In 1926, he formed a new political party called, Fianna Fail (*Soldiers of Destiny*) and in 1932, he was elected Taoiseach/President of the Executive Council of the Free State. The country ratified a new constitution under him on 29th December 1937.

It is said of de Valera that many years later in private conversation, he was asked if there, was any one thing he regretted in life, and it is reported he said: '*...not accepting the Treaty.*'

The declaration of the Irish Free State as an Independent Republic came into force on 18th April 1948, during the tenure of the inter-party government of Fine Gael (*Family of the Irish* or *Tribe of the Irish*) and Clann na Poblacha (*Family of the Republic*), the general opposition to de Valera's Fianna Fail Party, when Ireland ended all ties with the Commonwealth. The Taoiseach (Prime Minister) John A. Costello and his Fine Gael party were direct descendants of Michael Collins.

This declaration eventually turned the country from a constitutional monarchy into a republic, thus fulfilling Michael Collins' prediction of 'the freedom to achieve freedom.'

As in most civil wars, the internecine conflict left a bitter legacy which continues to influence Irish politics to this day. Until the 1970s, almost all of Ireland's prominent politicians were veterans of both sides of the Civil War, a fact which poisoned the relationships between Ireland's biggest parties, Fine Gael, under Richard Mulcahy, and Fianna Fail, under Eamon de Valera, all descendants of the Pro-Treaty and Anti-Treaty forces of 1922. Moreover, many of these men's sons and daughters also became politicians, meaning that the personal wounds of the civil war were felt over three generations.

The sad truth is the Anti-Treaty forces could never grasp the fact that freedom is a process, not just an idea or an ideal outcome, that progress is more important than perfection. Most people in Ireland today, including members of de Valera's own party, Fianna Fail, agree it was a mistake to oppose the Treaty and that it was the best deal on offer for the Irish at that time.

IRA

IRA (Irish Republican Army), the name given to the national force that fought the Anglo-Irish War 1919-1921, also known as the 'Troubles'. The IRA emerged out of the Irish Volunteer organization established in 1913, to exert pressure on the British Government to grant Home Rule for Ireland. After 1914, it was taken over by an older revolutionary nationalist organization, the Irish Republican Brotherhood (IRB), dedicated to the establishment of a unitary Irish Republic by armed conflict. In the 1916 Easter Rising the, rebel forces were declared to be the Army of the Irish Republic, but the term IRA did not come into use until after the Declaration of Independence in 1919. Officially, it remained Oglaich na nEireann (Irish Volunteers).

Under the leadership, of Michael Collins, Richard Mulcahy and Harry Boland, the traditional IRB policy of insurrection was replaced by a guerrilla strategy. The keynote was the local company or battalion; brigades (one to three per county) were shadowy formations, and the divisions introduced later in 1921 existed mainly on paper. Local energy in pursuit of weapons, skill in the use of explosives and determination to engage the British police and military forces, were indispensable. Volunteers had to sign the following enlistment form:

> '*I, the undersigned, desire to be enrolled for service in Ireland as a member of the Irish Volunteer Force. I subscribe to the Constitution of the Irish Volunteers and pledge my willing*

obedience to every article of it. I declare that in joining the Irish Volunteer Force I set before myself the stated objects of the Irish Volunteers and no others.

1. To secure and maintain the rights and liberties common to all peoples of Ireland.

2. To train, discipline and equip for this purpose an Irish Volunteer Force which will render service to the Irish National Government when such is established.

3. To unite in the service of Ireland Irishmen of every creed and every party and class.'

The IRA campaign impelled the British Government to negotiate, but could not compel it to concede full Irish Independence. When the Anglo-Irish Treaty was signed, accepting partition and non-republican status for the Irish Free State, a number of local IRA commanders believed that they could still fight on to achieve a unitary Republic. The split over the issue and the Civil War followed. Defeat in the Civil War reduced the IRA to sporadic attempts to restart its campaign, and being declared illegal by the Irish Government in 1931.

It is important to differentiate between the 'Old IRA' and the various splinter-groups, the 'Official' IRA – The 'Provisional' IRA – The 'Real' IRA – The 'Continuity' IRA, i.e. the groups formed in, and after, the late 1960s in the wake of the anti-Catholic pogroms, riots and murders in Northern Ireland.

The eruption of conflict in Northern Ireland in 1969 found the 'Official IRA' unprepared and in 1971, a breakaway group, the Provisional IRA (PIRA), returned to the traditional policy of force. After a campaign lasting 25 years, it reversed its long-standing repudiation of politics declaring a cessation of operations to allow its political wing Sinn Fein, to participate in constitutional negotiations. They produced the Good Friday Agreement (1998), in which the IRA agreed to decommission (disarm). In July 2002, the PIRA announced that it was ending its armed struggle and instead would pursue peaceful means to achieve its objectives.

'War does not determine who is right—only who is left.'
(Bertrand Russell)

CONFLICT

*And whereas for seven hundred years the Irish people has
never ceased to repudiate and has repeatedly protested in arms
against foreign usurpation.*
(Unknown)

Every conflict is subject to what preceded it and in the case of
the struggle for a free and independent Ireland, by 1914, that
struggle was over seven hundred years old.

It started back in May 1169, when a force of 30 knights, 60 arms
men and 300 bowmen landed at Bannow Bay, County Wexford,
followed by a further ten knights and sixty bowmen. This force
merged with some 500 soldiers under the command of Diarmait
mac Murchadha the ousted King of Leinster. Marching towards
Wexford they were confronted by Gaels in the first battle to stop
foreigners invading Ireland and the first bloody encounter in what
was to become an ongoing struggle for the next seven hundred
years. Following an attack in which eighteen of the enemy were
killed and three of the defenders, Wexford and the surrounding
baronies of Forth and Bargy fell to the invaders.

1171, King Henry II of England landed at Crook, near Waterford,
with a large army and in a short time, Leinster was conquered, with
Henry establishing his headquarters in Dublin. Pope Alexander III
wrote to Henry praising him on his conquest of Ireland.

1177, Prince John was appointed Lord of all Ireland, and in 1185, he was sent to govern the country, granting unconquered Irish lands to Norman chiefs who built castles at Lismore and Ardfinnan.

1186, is the first recorded case of insurrection; Hugh de Lacy was assassinated after he erected a castle on the site of Durrow Monastery, and so rebellion started.

1339, The Dublin Annals stated that there was *'general war throughout Ireland'*.

1358, Art MacMurrough raised war in Leinster and threatened Dublin.

1534, 'Silken Thomas' Fitzgerald rebelled against Henry VIII and attacked Dublin Castle.

1598, Rebellion broke out throughout Ireland. Resistance was led by Hugh O'Neill and lasted over nine years. The Irish chieftains were finally defeated, which lead to their exile (the Flight of the Earls), leading to the Plantation of Ulster.

1599. A notable victory. A detachment of the army of the Lord Lieutenant, The Earl of Essex, was set upon by Owney O'More of Lois near the village of Timahoe. The site became known as the 'Pass of The Plumes' on account of the number of plumes from English helmets left on the ground. Some 5000 English soldiers were killed.

1603, Some 50,000 Irish people, including Irish prisoners of the Nine Years War, were sold as indentured labourers to English colonies in America, and the West Indies.

1606:

> '*Scots were allowed to settle in Ulster as part of the Ulster Plantation Plan. These settlers were predominantly Presbyterians who feared Catholics. The English government encouraged this settlement because it helped them control Ireland economically and socially, as settlers imposed "civilized" values on the Irish "barbarians."*
>
> *As English settlers continued to arrive in Ireland, they took much of the best farmland for themselves. As a result, most Irish farmers and herdsmen saw their status continually diminished and deeply resented the occupiers.'*

(*101 Things you Didn't Know about Irish History*, Ryan Hackney & Amy Hackney Blackwell.)

1641, Rebellion broke out among the Irish population of Ulster. At this stage, Irish Catholics still owned 59% of Irish land.

1642, In the summer, the Catholic upper classes formed the Catholic Federation, which became the government of Ireland, until 1664, where, in the Cromwellian conquest of Ireland, the Catholic landowners were permanently dispossessed of their lands.

1649, Oliver Cromwell landed in Dublin with thirty-five ships full of troops and equipment. To be followed by his henchman Henry Ireton with an additional seventy-seven ships. Cromwell marched on Drogheda which was garrisoned by 3000 troops under the command of Arthur Ashton. When the invaders took the town by storm, they massacred the garrison, all Catholic priests and many civilians. Ashton was beaten to death with his own wooden leg.

Moving on to Wexford Cromwell sacked it, putting 2000 soldiers and 15000 townspeople to the sword. He carried on in this way until 1650, his reconquest of Ireland being brutal in the extreme. The war he started included the wholesale burning of crops, forced population movement (ethnic cleansing), the killing of civilians and a resulting famine throughout the country all of which was responsible for an estimated 600,000 Irish deaths out of a population of 1,400,000. It destroyed the native Irish Catholic land-owing class to be replaced by colonists from Britain, and Cromwell's soldiers who were entitled to a grant of confiscated land in lieu of wages that parliament was unable to pay in full. The bitterness of the Cromwellian settlements became a powerful source of Irish nationalism from then on. He is still a much hated man in Ireland.

1688, The percentage of land now owned by Irish Catholics had shrunk to 22%. By 1706, only 18% of Irish land remained in Catholic ownership. This situation was brought about by the continuing insertion of a community from Britain during the time of the Plantations, in which lands held by Gaelic Irish clans were confiscated and given to Protestant settlers ('Planters') from England and Scotland. In the Plantation of Ulster, the province was heavily colonized with English and Scottish Settlers. The newcomers were given land and opportunities that were denied to the native Irish, and they were always under threat from the dispossessed and their descendants.

1690, July 1. The Battle of the Boyne was fought between two rival claimants of the English, Scottish and Irish thrones, Catholic King James and the Protestant King William III, who had deposed James, had landed at Carrickfergus with a 36,000-strong army, over 40 pieces of artillery and a war chest of £20,000 in cash.

For the Jacobites, (Irish Catholic supporters of James II) led by Richard Talbot, 1st Earl of Tyrconnel, the war was fought for Irish sovereignty, religious toleration for Catholicism, and land ownership. The Catholic upper classes had lost almost all their lands after Cromwell's conquest of Ireland, as well as the right to hold public office, practice their religion, and sit in the Irish parliament. They saw the Catholic King James as the means of redressing these grievances and securing autonomy of Ireland from England. It is sad to note that the battle was the first victory for the League of Augsburg, the first-ever alliance between Catholic and Protestant countries, with Pope Alexander VIII and William of Orange the League's prime movers.

1714, Dr Hugh MacMahon, bishop of Clogher reported that the greatest problem for the Catholic community in Ulster was its poverty:

> *'Although all Ireland is suffering, this province is worse off than the rest of the country because of the fact that the neighbouring country of Scotland's Presbyterians are coming over here daily in large groups of families, occupying the towns and villages, seizing the farms in the richer parts of the country and expelling the natives... The result is that the Catholic natives are forced to build their huts in mountainous or marshy country.'*

1775, Henry Grattan became the leader of the Irish Patriot Party, and in 1780, he proposed legislative independence for Ireland which was rejected.

1795, The United Irishmen led by Theobald Wolfe Tone, an iconic figure in Irish nationalism, born at 44 Stafford Street, Dublin, the son of a coach maker, turned itself into a secret society dedicated to the military overthrow of English power.

The issue of freedom was an important part of their ideology.

The Declaration of the United Irishmen, written by Wolfe Tone, contained the following statements regarding the government of Ireland:

'We have no national Government – we are ruled by Englishmen and the servants of Englishmen whose object is the interest of another country, whose instrument is corruption, and whose strength is the weakness of Ireland... Such an extreme power, acting with uniform force, in a direction too frequently opposite to the true line of our obvious interests, can be resisted with effect solely by unanimity, decision and spirit of the people.' (Theobald Wolfe Tone, Declaration of the United Irishmen.)

On 23rd May **1798**, The Irish Rebellion occurred with the first clashes taking place in County Kildare on 24th May, before spreading out through Leinster and other areas of the country thereafter. French soldiers landed in Ireland and participated in the rebellion. The French also came ashore at Killala on 22nd August where they were defeated, to be followed by the massacres of Irish Catholics in Dunlavin and Carnew.

'Can you think of entering into a treaty with a British Minister? A minister too, who has left you at the mercy of English soldiery, who has laid your cities to waste, and massacred inhumanely your best citizens...'

(General James Napper Tandy, leader of the uprising. His proclamation 'Liberty or Death'.)

Wolfe Tone was captured and sentenced to be hanged and not shot as a soldier, as he wished. In defiance he cut his own throat, dying a week later from the wound.

1801, January 1; Act of Union. Ireland became an integral part of the United Kingdom.

1803, Robert Emmet planned an insurrection:

'You are now called on to show to the world that you are competent to take your place among nations, that you have a right to claim their recognizance of you, as an independent country... We therefore solemnly declare, that our object is to establish a free and independent republic of Ireland: that the pursuit of this object we will relinquish only with our lives... We war against no religious sect... We war against English dominion.' (Robert Emmet, *Proclamation of the Provisional Government.*)

'He and his followers marched on Dublin Castle in an attempt to seize it by force, but the army dispersed them. Emmet escaped and was later arrested on the 25 August and executed by hanging in Dublin, on the 20th September 1803.

*The story of his house-keeper Anne Devlin, whom he hired to make his home like an ordinary suburban establishment, rather than the hot-bed of subversion it was, indicates the savagery that prevailed at the time, and which was to be repeated time and again in the future. Anne was arrested and tortured for information following Emmett's failed uprising. She was repeatedly hanged to the point of unconsciousness, then revived for another round of torture. Through all this, and despite offers of substantial bribes, she refused to talk. Even when Emmett told her that betraying him would do no harm, as he was about to be hanged anyway. She survived the ordeal, only to die in anonymous squalor in the 1840's'.

'An Gorta Mor, the Great Potato famine, is one of the pivotal events in Irish history. Millions emigrated, and the resulting demographic shift led to a decreasing population. The famine also ignited anger against the British government, which eventually grew into the Irish independence movement.'*

(*101 Things You Didn't Know about Irish History*, Ryan Hackney & Amy Hackney Blackwell.)

The Great Famine had a massive impact on Ireland. Some in Ireland believed the government in London – to solve the 'Irish Problem' – had deliberately done as little as possible to aid the people of Ireland – a form of genocide – and these people concluded the only hope Ireland had for its future was a complete separation from Britain. If London was unwilling to grant this then they would fight for it.

In **1848**, this, anger spilled over as a group of revolutionaries known as Young Ireland launched an ill-prepared uprising against the government. Which failed.

In **1858**, James Stephens founded the Irish Republican Brotherhood (IRB), or the The Fenians, in Dublin and New York, which included Micheal Doheny, Charles Kirkham, John O'Leary, Thomas Clarke Luby and John O'Mahony. They had one simple desire for Ireland – independence from British rule. They organised the movement along the lines of circles which was comparative to a regiment. It was very secretive with each rank only knowing the one above it. They also established themselves in Australia and Canada. A Fenian uprising, planned for March 1866, was betrayed and failed miserably; then an attempted uprising in 1867 led by Thomas Kelly, who had fought in the American Civil War. He and another Fenian attempted an attack on Chester Castle to gain weapons and ammunition. This was not successful and Kelly and his companion were arrested. However, the activity of the Fenians was partly responsible for spurring William Gladstone into his stated mission '*to pacify Ireland*'. This led to the rise of Home Rule and the issues surrounding it.

1873, Sir Isaac Butt founded the Home Rule League in Manchester and Dublin and in 1874, his motion for Home Rule in Ireland, independence from the United Kingdom, limited self-government, was defeated in the British House of Commons.

1886, The Irish Catholic Hierarchy formally endorsed Home Rule. From then on Ireland was dominated by the Irish pursuit of Home Rule, with subsequent motions being defeated regularly. William Gladstone introduced the First Home Rule Bill in the House of Commons. It failed to get a majority.

1893, Second Home Rule Bill. It was vetoed by the House of Lords.

1912, Third Home Rule Bill introduced by Lloyd George.

1914, Third Home Rule Bill placed on the Statute Book, but its implementation was suspended until the end of the Great War.

From the first invasion of Ireland by the English, they treated the Irish as an inferior race. The English worked on the principle that, as the Irish were worth nothing, they deserved nothing. This attitude was most strongly expressed during the Famine when they let thousands of Irish die of hunger while exporting tons of grain and wheat, grown in Ireland, to England and abroad. In the following extraordinary passage, British Prime Minster Lord Salisbury recognised the Irish people had valid cause for harbouring a deep sense of being wronged when he wrote:

> '...governed by men of an alien race and alien creed, persecuted because they clung to their fathers' faith and avowed the blood that flowed in their veins, stripped of their property by the invaders, fettered in their trade that their masters might prosper, crushed by unequal laws, harnessed by degrading disabilities, galled, depressed and disheartened

by the open, never-abating scorn of the race that had conquered them.'

So, this seemingly endless armed struggle for human freedom and social justice, dominated by counter narrative ever reluctant to grant the rebels either stature or voice was to continue.

'There was never born an Englishman who understands the Irish People.'
(Bernadette Devlin)

THE ANGLO IRISH TREATY

(An Conradh Angla – Eireannach)

1,737 words that spelled freedom for Ireland

1. Ireland shall have the same constitutional status in the Community of Nations known as the British Empire as the Dominion of Canada, the Commonwealth of Australia, the Dominion of New Zealand, and the Union of South Africa with a Parliament having powers to make laws for the peace order of good government of Ireland and an Executive responsible to that parliament, and shall be styled and known as the Irish Free State.

2. Subject to the provisions hereinafter set out the positions of the Irish Free State in relation to the Imperial Parliament and Government and otherwise shall be of that of the Dominion of Canada, and the law, practice and constitutional usage governing the relationship of the Crown or the representative of the Crown and of the Imperial Parliament to the Dominion of Canada shall govern their relationship to the Irish Free State.

3. The representative of the Crown in Ireland shall be appointed in like manner as the Governor-General of Canada and in

accordance with the practice observed in the making of such appointments.

4. The oath to be taken by members of the parliament of the Irish Fee State shall be in the following form:-

    I......do solemnly swear true faith and allegiance to the Constitution of the Irish Free State as by law established and that I will be faithful to H.M. King George V., his heirs and successors by law, in virtue of the common citizenship of Ireland with Great Britain and her adherence to and membership of the group of nations forming the British Commonwealth of Nations.

5. The Irish Free State shall assume liability for the service of the Public Debt of the United Kingdom as existing as the date hereof and towards of payment of War Pensions as existing as the date in such proportion as may be fair and equitable, having regard to any just claim on the part the of Ireland by way of set-off or counter claim, the amount of such sums being determined in default of agreement by the arbitration of one or more independent persons being citizens of the British Empire.

6. Until an arrangement has been made between the British and Irish Governments whereby the Irish Free State undertakes her own coastal defence, the defence of sea of Great Britain and Ireland shall be undertaken by His Majesty's Imperial Forces, but this shall not prevent the construction or maintenance by the Government of the Irish Free State of such vessels as are necessary for the protection of the Revenues or the Fisheries. The foregoing provisions of this article shall be reviewed at a Conference of Representatives of the British and Irish governments, to be held at the expiration of five years from the date hereof with a view to a share in her own coastal defence.

7. The Government of the Irish Free State shall afford to His Majesty's Imperial Forces:

    (a) In the time of peace such harbour and other facilities as are indicated in the Annex hereto, or such other facilities as may from time to time be agreed between the British Government and the Government of the Irish Free State;

    (b) In time of war or of strained relations with a Foreign Power such harbour and other facilities as the British Government may require for the purpose of such defence as aforesaid.

8. With a view to securing the observance of the principle of international limitation of armaments if the Government of the Irish Free State establishes and maintains a military defence force, the establishments thereof shall not exceed in size such proportion of the military establishes maintained in Great Britain as that which the population of Ireland bears to the population of Great Britain.

9. The ports of Great Britain and the Irish Free State shall be freely open to ships of the other country on payment of the customary port and other dues.

10. The Government of the Irish Free State agrees to pay fair compensation on terms not less favourable than those accorded by the act of 1920 to judges, officials, members of Police Forces and other Public Servants who are discharged by it or who retire in consequence of the change in government effected in pursuance hereof. Provided that the agreement shall not apply to members of Auxiliary Police Force or persons recruited in Great Britain for the Royal Irish

Constabulary during the two years next preceding the date hereof. The British Government will assume responsibility for such compensation or pensions as may be payable to any of these excepted persons.

11. Until the expiration of one month from the passing of the Act of Parliament for the ratification of this instrument, the powers of the Parliament and the Government of the Irish Free State shall not be exercisable as respects Northern Ireland, and the provisions of the Government of Ireland act 1920, shall, as far as they relate to Northern Ireland remain of full force and effect, and no election shall be held for the return of members to serve in the parliament of the Irish Free State for constituencies in Northern Ireland, unless a resolution is passed by both Houses of Parliament of Northern Ireland in favour of holding such election before the end of the said month.

12. If before the expiration of the said month, an address is presented to His Majesty by both Houses of Parliament of Northern Ireland that effect, the powers of the Parliament and Government of the Irish Free State shall no longer extend to Northern Ireland, and the provisions of the Government of Ireland Act 1920 (including those relating to the Council of Ireland) shall so far as they relate to Northern Ireland, continue to be of full force and effect, and this instrument shall have effect subject to the necessary modifications. Provided that if such an address is so presented a Commission consisting of three persons, one to be appointed by the Irish Free State, one to be appointed by the Government of Northern Ireland, and one who shall be Chairman to be

appointed by the British Government shall determine in accordance with the wishes of the inhabitants, so far as may be compatible with economic and geographic conditions the boundaries between Northern Ireland and the rest of Ireland, and for the purposes of the Government of Ireland Act, 1920. And of this instrument, the boundary of Northern Ireland shall be such as may be determined by such Commission.

13. For the purpose of the last foregoing article, the powers of the Parliament of Southern Ireland under the Government of Ireland Act 1920 to elect members of the council of Ireland shall after the parliament of the Irish Fee State is constituted be exercised by that Parliament.

14. After the expiration of the said month, if no such address as is mentioned in Article 12 hereof is presented, the Parliament and Government of Northern Ireland shall continue to exercise as respects Northern Ireland the powers conferred on them by the Government of Ireland Act, 1920, but the Parliament and Government of the Irish Free State shall in Northern Ireland have a relation to matters in respect of which the Parliament of Northern Ireland has not power to make laws under the Act (including matters under the said Act are within the jurisdiction of the Council of Ireland) the same powers as in the rest of Ireland, subject to such other provisions as may be agreed in manner hereinafter appearing.

15. At any time after the date hereof the Government of Northern Ireland and the provisional Government of Southern Ireland hereinafter constituted may meet for the purpose of discussing the provisions subject to which the last

foregoing Article is to operate in the event of no such address as is herein mentioned being presented and those provisions may include:-

(a) Safeguards with regard to patronage in Northern Ireland

(b) Safeguards with regard to the collection of revenue in Northern Ireland

(c) Safeguards with regard to import and export duties affecting the trade or industry of Northern Ireland.

(d) Safeguards as for the minorities in Northern Ireland

(e) The settlement of financial relations between Northern Ireland and the Irish Free State.

(f) The establishment and powers of a local militia in Northern Ireland and the relation of the Defence Forces of the Irish Free State and of Northern Ireland respectively, and if at any such meeting provisions are agreed to, the same shall have effect as if they were included amongst the provisions subject to which the powers of Parliament and the Government of the Irish Free State are to be exercisable in Northern Ireland under Article 14 hereof.

16. Neither the parliament of the Irish Free State nor the Parliament of Northern Ireland shall make any law so as either directly or indirectly to endow any religion or prohibit or restrict the free exercise thereof or give any preference or impose any disability on account of religious belief or religious status or affect prejudicially the right of any child to attend a school receiving public money without attending religious instruction at the school or make any discrimination as

respects State aid between schools under the management of different religious denominations or divert from any religious denomination or any educational institution any of its property except for public utility purposes and on payment of compensation.

17. By way of provisional arrangement for the administration of Southern Ireland during the interval which must elapse between the date hereof and the constitution of a Parliament and Government of the Irish Free State in accordance therewith, steps shall be taken forthwith for summoning a meeting of members of Parliament elected for constituencies in Southern Ireland since the passing of the Government of Ireland Act 1920, and for constituting a provisional Government, and the British Government shall take the steps necessary to transfer such provisional Government, the powers and machinery requisite for the discharge of its duties, provided that every member of such provisional Government shall have signified in writing his or her acceptance of this instrument. But this arrangement shall not continue in force beyond the expiration of twelve months from the date hereof.

18. This instrument shall be submitted forthwith by His Majesty's Government for the approval of Parliament and by the Irish signatories to a meeting summoned for the purpose of the member elected to sit in the House of Commons of Southern Ireland and if approved shall be ratified by necessary legislation.

On behalf of the British Delegation.	On behalf of The Irish Delegation.
Signed :	Signed:
David Lloyd George MP (Prime Minister)	Art O Griobhtha (Arthur Griffith)
Austen Chamberlain	Micheal O Coileain (Michael Collins)
Birkenhead (Lord)	Riobard Bartun (Robert Barton)
Winston S. Churchill	Eudhmonn S. O Dugain
L. Worthington-Evans	(Edmund J Duggan)
Sir Gordon Hewart	Seorsa Ghabhain Ui Dhubhthaig.
	(George Gavan Duffy)

6th December 1921.

Footnote: Robert Barton, who represented Kildare/Wicklow, stated that the Treaty was the *'lesser of two outrages forced upon him'*. He later rejected the Treaty and committed himself to the Irish Republic.

The Treaty's main clauses were that:

- British Forces would withdraw from 26 Counties of Ireland.

- Ireland to become a self-governing dominion of the British Empire.

- The British Monarch would be the Head of State of the Irish Free State and would be represented by a Governor General, as a Representative of the Crown.

- Members of the new Free State parliament to take an Oath of Allegiance. A part of the Oath was to: *'be faithful to His Majesty King George V., his heirs and successor by law, in virtue of the common citizenship'*

- Northern Ireland to have the option of withdrawing from the Irish Free State within one month of the Treaty coming into effect. If Northern Ireland chose to withdraw, a Boundary

Commission would be constituted to draw the boundary between the Irish Free State and Northern Ireland.

- Britain would continue to control a limited number of ports, to be known as the Treaty Ports, for the Royal Navy.
- The Irish Free State to assume responsibility for its part of the Imperial Debt.

The Treaty to give superior status in Irish Law and take precedence in the event of a conflict between it and the new 1922 Constitution of the Irish Free State.

THE MACHINE GUN CORPS

Army Council Instructions, No 1589, dated 14th August 1916

'It has been represented that many men have been selected for the Machine Gun Corps who have been found physically unfit for work required of that Corps. The physical standard required for a man in the MGC is shown below, and no man should be appointed who does not attain this standard.

a   *General Physique. The all-round standard required as a machine gunner is far higher than that necessary for an infantry soldier. To be well developed and sufficiently strongly built to enable him to work with, and carry, a machine gun/similar weight under adverse conditions, and if necessary, to double [run] or crawl with it. He must have no physical defects, which would interfere with this work.*

b   *Age. Not less than 19 years, not over 35 years, but the actual age is not so important as the general physical condition of the individual.*

c   *Height. Not less than 5 ft 3 in exceptional cases.*

d.   *Chest measurement. Range of expansion not to be less than 3 ins, but 3 ins is sufficient for untrained recruits.*

e.   *Eyesight. Without glasses V=6/9 with at least one eye.'*

The Machine Gun Corps machine gunners were nicknamed 'The Suicide Club,' as they were the object of very special attention by enemy artillery and snipers.

THE VICKERS MACHINE GUN (MARK 1/V/11)

(Photograph is courtesy of the Imperial War Museum)

The weapon George went to war with was the Vickers Machine Gun (Mark 1/V11), known as the Emma Gee (from the phonetic alphabet of the time for the letters MG). It was adopted by the British Army in 1912, and earned an enviable reputation for reliability and effectiveness as a support weapon. It had to be water cooled; the jacket holding 7 ½ pints / 4.25 litres of coolant that boiled after 600 rounds (bullets) were fired. The steam collected in a condensing can and re-used to refill the water jacket. It was capable of firing 10,000 rounds per hour, when the barrel had to be changed.

This took a trained team about two minutes, without loss of fluid from the water jacket. The gunner, a highly trained soldier, was able to deal with breakdowns, stoppages and major repairs in a matter of minutes. Sometimes, when pushed, he could restore the gun in ten to twelve seconds. For this, the team carried a bag of spares from which they could almost build another gun. The ammunition came in wooden boxes ready belted, or in cardboard boxes of 100 rounds which hand fed, into the special canvas belts with the use of a mechanical loading device. The maximum rate of fire per minute exceeded that of fifty expert riflemen. It is no exaggeration to say the machine gun played the most conspicuous part in the Great War. To it must be allotted the premier place among the death dealing instruments of modern warfare. The Gunner, who became a light-fingered expert, could fire just one shot or two when needed to conserve ammunition. A gun team consisted of six men. No.1, a Lance Corporal in charge fired the gun and carried the tripod, No. 2 fed in the 250 round canvas belts into the weapon and carried the gun barrel and No. 3 supplied ammo to the gun. The rest of the team were employed as range finders; it was their job to prepare highly accurate range cards for the guns in front of the outpost lines. They also had the job of carrying ammunition and spares. All this, along with a full pack on their backs. Numbers 1 and 2 were armed with six shot revolvers. The Colt, Smith & Wesson and Webley revolvers were all issued to gun teams. Numbers 3, 4 and 5 had Lee-Enfield rifles as their personal weapons. The rifle was difficult to manage as well as the rest of their awkward and heavy loads.

KITCHENER

Field Marshal Horatio Herbert (Lord) Kitchener, 1st Earl of Khartoum, was appointed Secretary of War, for the First World at the outbreak of hostilities with Germany. As a recruiting officer, for the New Armies he had great success with his finger-pointing picture on recruiting posters, one of the most famous images of the 20th century. He was born near Ballylongford, Co. Kerry, Ireland in 1850, and drowned, along with 642 sailors and soldiers when the cruiser *HMS Hampshire* struck a mine off the Orkney's on 5th June 1916.

FIELD PUNISHMENT NO: 1

If one is of the opinion that the 28 days Field Punishment No:1 George received in Salonika was pretty harsh, then spare a thought for Private Patrick Joseph Downey:

Patrick, the son of Michael and Mary Downey of Vizes Fields, County Limerick, gave his age as 18 years when he enlisted in August 1914; it has been said he lied about this and was just 16 years old. He joined the 5th (Extra Reserve) Munster Regiment and transferred to the 6th Bn, Leinsters (George's Regiment). It was possible George knew him, but it is certain that he knew about him. He had fought in the hell hole of Gallipoli and had now been in action against the Bulgarians, for about two months, in a deadly cold winter in Greece.

His disciplinary record suggests that he was less than a model soldier, given to losing equipment, ignoring battalion orders and other petty offences. He had recently been charged with insubordination and sentenced to 84 days Field Punishment No:1.

When his cap, which he had to wear while tied in an X-formation to a gun carriage wheel, fell into the mud, he was ordered by an officer to put the cap, now soaking wet and covered with muck, back on his head, but he twice refused. He was charged with disobedience and brought before a Field General Court Martial. No provision was made to ensure he had a defending officer, and, undefended, he pleaded guilty to the charge.

Private Patrick Joseph Downey was 'Shot at Dawn' on Monday 27th December 1915 at Eurenjik, near the port of Salonika. His death was reported to have been instantaneous.

HISTORY OF ATHLONE

Athlone is at the heart of Ireland, geographically and historically. The ford of Athlone was strategically important, as south of the town the River Shannon is passable until Clonmacnoise, where the Esker Riada meets the Shannon.

In 1001 Brian Boru, High King of all Ireland, led his army from Kincora to Athlone, his fleet sailing upriver via Lough Derg.

A bridge was built across the river in the 12th century, south of the current bridge. To protect this, a fort was built on the west bank by Turloch O'Connor. On a number of occasions, both the fort and bridge were subjected to attacks, and towards the end of the century the Anglo-Normans constructed a motte-and-bailey fortification there. This was superseded by a stone structure built in 1210, by Justiciar John Gray. The 12-sided donjon dates from this time. The rest was destroyed during the Siege of Athlone and subsequently rebuilt and enlarged.

The current battlements and cannon emplacements were installed to prevent a French fleet from sailing up the Shannon and establishing a bridgehead in Lough Ree, likewise at Shannonbridge, near Clonmacnoise. It was later damaged by a lightning strike on the powder store. The two mortars situated in front of the donjon are believed to date to the Williamite wars, and were previously located outside the main entrance to Custume barracks. The idea, mooted during the Elizabethan wars, of relocating the Lord Deputy of Ireland here from Dublin, illustrated the strategic importance of the town. During the wars that racked Ireland in the seventeenth century, the town held a vital position, holding the main bridge over the River Shannon into Connacht. In the Irish Confederate Wars 1641-1653, the town was held by Irish Confederate troops until it was taken in the late 1650s by Charles Coote, who attacked the town from the west, having crossed into Connacht at Sligo.

Forty years later, during the Williamite War known as An Cogadh an Da Ri, War of the Two Kings, between King William of Orange and King James II of the house of Stuart, the town was again the centre of strategic importance, being one of the Jacobite strongholds defending their position having retreated west after the Battle of the Boyne. At the First Battle of Athlone in 1690, the Jacobite forces of Colonel Richard Grace repelled an attack by 10,000 men led by Commander Douglas. The following year, the Siege of Athlone saw a further assault in which troops of King William III eventually prevailed against the outnumbered defenders.

The current bridge was built in the 19th century to replace the old bridge which was becoming dangerous to the increasing traffic. Originally, the bridge had a moveable section which was decommissioned in the mid-20th century.

IN CONCLUSION

On 17th of May 2011, Queen Elizabeth II and her Consort, Prince Philip, Duke of Edinburgh paid a State Visit to Ireland. On that day, along with Irish President Mary McAleese, they visited the Garden of Remembrance dedicated to the memory of all those who gave their lives in the cause of Irish Freedom. There the queen placed a wreath at the foot of the Children of Lir sculpture and bowed her head in homage to the freedom fighters from the many uprisings who helped break the link with the crown and gain freedom for the Irish Nation.

Then, on 18th of May 2011, the queen visited The Irish National War Memorial at Islandbridge, Dublin, to lay a wreath at the Great Cross of Sacrifice and pay homage and tribute to the thousands of brave and gallant Irishmen who fell fighting in British uniforms in the Great War.

That evening, at a state banquet, the queen made the following speech:

'A hUachtartrain agus a chairde (president and friends).

Prince Philip and I are delighted to be here, and experience at first hand Ireland's world famous hospitality.

Together we have much to celebrate: the ties between our two people, the shared values, and the economic, business and cultural links that make us so much more than neighbours, that make us firm friends and equal partners.

Madame President, speaking here in Dublin Castle it is impossible to ignore the weight of history, as it was yesterday when you and I laid wreaths at the Garden of Remembrance.

Indeed so much of this visit reminds us of the complexity of our history, its many layers and traditions, but also the importance of forbearance and conciliation, of being able to bow to the past but not be bound to it.

Of course the relationship has not always been straightforward; nor has the record over the centuries been entirely benign.

It is a sad and regrettable reality that through history our islands have experienced more than their fair share of heartache, turbulence and loss.

These events have touched us all, many of us personally, and are a painful legacy.

We can never forget those who have died or been injured or their families.

To all those who have suffered as a consequence of our troubled past I extend my sincere thoughts and deep sympathy.

With the benefit of historical hindsight we can all see things which we would wish had been done differently or not at all.

But it is also true that no one who looked to the future over past centuries could have imagined that strength of the bonds that are now in place between the governments and the people of our two nations, the spirit of partnership that we now enjoy, and the lasting rapport between us.

No one here this evening could doubt the heartfelt desire of our two nations.

Madame President, you have done a great deal to promote this understanding and reconciliation. You set out to build bridges. And I have seen at first hand, your success in bringing together different communities and traditions on this island.

You have shed new light on the sacrifices of those who served in the First World War.

Even as we jointly opened Messines Peace Park in 1998 it was difficult to look ahead to a time when you and I would be standing together at Islandbridge as we were today.

That transformation is also evident in the establishment of a successful power-sharing executive in Northern Ireland. A knot of history that was painstakingly loosened by the British and Irish Governments together with the strength, vision and determination of political parties in Northern Ireland.

What were once only hopes for the future have now come to pass; it is almost 13 years since the overwhelming majority of people in Ireland and Northern Ireland voted in favour of the agreement signed on Good Friday 1998, paving the way for Northern Ireland to become the exciting and inspirational place that it is today.

I applaud the work of all those involved in the peace process and all of those who support and nurture the peace, including the members of the police, the Garda and the other emergency services, and those who work in the communities, the Churches and charitable bodies like Co-operation Ireland.

Taken together, their work not only serves as the basis for reconciliation between our peoples and communities, but is gives hope to other peacemakers across the world that through sustained effort, peace can and will prevail.

For the world moves on quickly. The challenges of the past have been replaced by new economic challenges which will demand the same imagination and courage.

The lesson from the peace process is clear—whatever life throws at us, our individual responses will be all the stronger for working together and sharing the load.

There are other stories written daily across these islands which do not find their voice in solemn pages of history books, or newspaper headlines but which are at the heart of shared narrative.

Many British families have members who live in this country, as many Irish families have close relatives in the United Kingdom. These families share the two islands; they have visited each other and have come home to each other over the years.

They are the ordinary people who yearned for the peace and understanding we now have between our two nations and between communities within those two nations; a living testament to how much in common we have.

These ties of family, friendship and affection are our most precious resource. They are the lifeblood of the partnership across these islands, a golden thread that runs through all our joint successes so far, and all we will go on to achieve.

They are a reminder that we have much to do together to build a future for all our grandchildren; the kind of future our grandparents could only dream of.

So we celebrate together the widespread spirit of goodwill and deep mutual understanding that has served to make the relationship more harmonious, close as good neighbours should always be.'

BIBLIOGRAPHY

Bartlett, Thomas & Jeffery, Keith:
(1996) *A Military History of Ireland*,
Cambridge University Press,
Cambridge, England. UK.

Corley, Finian:
(2003) *Ambush at Auburn*, Journal of the Old
Athlone Society. Athlone,
Co. Westmeath, Republic of Ireland.

Cox, Liam:
(1981) *Moate County Westmeath* (A History
of the Town and the District),
Alfa Print Limited, Athlone,
Co. Westmeath, Republic of Ireland

Crutchley, C E:
(1973) *Machine Gunner 1914-1918*, Pen &
Sword Books Ltd. Barnsley, Yorkshire, England. UK

Drum Heritage Group
(1994) *Drum & Its Heritage*
Alfa Print Limited, Athlone,
Co. Westmeath, Republic of Ireland

Egan, Frank:
(1980) *Bridging the Gap (Athlone's Golden Mile)*
(Paperback) Publisher: Frank Egan
Athlone, Co. Westmeath
Republic of Ireland.

Grainger, John D:
(2006) *The Battle for Palestine*
Boydell & Brewer Ltd.
Woodbridge, Suffolk, UK.

Hackney, Ryan & Hackney Blackwell, Amy:
(2007) *101 Things you didn't know about Irish History*
Adams Media Corp.
Avon Massachusetts, USA.

Hatton, S.F:
(1090) *The Yarn of a Yeoman*
Hutchinson & Co. (Publishers) Ltd.
34-36 Paternoster Row
London E.C.4

Hegarty Thorne, Kathleen:
(2005) *They Put The Flag a – Flyin*,
The Roscommon Volunteers,
Generation Organisation, Eugune, Oregon, USA.

Hemstead, Frank & Foy, Geoffrey:
(1994) *A Life in the flood plain of The River Shannon*, (Paperback)
Publishers, F. Hemstead & G. Foy. Athlone, Republic of Ireland.

Luxford, J.H. Maj:

(2004) *With the Machine Gunners in France*
& Palestine,
Naval & Military Press Ltd.
Unit 10 Ridgewood Ind. Est.
Uckfield, East Sussex,
England, UK.

Mageean, John:

(1945) *Man of the People,*
(The Story of Sean MacEoin.)
The Wood Printing Works Ltd
Wolfe Tone Street, Dublin,
Republic of Ireland.

O'Callaghan, Michael:

Irish and Freedom,
Roscommon Herald, Boyle
Roscommon.
Co. Roscommon,
Republic of Ireland.

O'Farrell, Padraic:

(1969) *Who's Who in the Irish War of*
Independence 1916-1922,
(1981) *The Sean MacEoin Story*
Mercier Publishing, Cork, Eire.

O'Meara, Seamus:
(1970) *Some Activities in Westmeath–1920*
Capuchin Annual, 1970.
Capuchin Publications, England,

Price, G. Ward:
The Story of the Salonika Army.

Pritchard, David:
(2001) *Chronology of Irish History,*
Lagan Books. Scotland. UK

Shea, Patrick:
(1981) *Voices and the Sound of Drums.*
An Irish Biography.
Blackstaff Press Publishers Ltd.
3 Galway Park, Dundonald
Belfast, Northern Ireland.

Stanley, Jeremy:
(2002) *Irelands Forgotten 10th*
Impact Printing Ltd,
Ballycastle Colraine.
Northern Ireland.

Wakefield, Alan & Moody, Simon:
(2004) *Under the Devils's Eye,*
Britain's Forgotten Army at Salonika
1915-1918, The History Press Ltd.

Westmeath Independent
(1960) *The Take-Over of Victoria
Barracks, Athlone.*
Westmeath Independent
Sean Costello Street
Athlone, Co. Westmeath,
Republic of Ireland.

White, G. & O'Shea, B:
(2003*) Irish Volunteer Soldier,*
Osprey Publishing
Botley, Oxford, UK

Woodward, David. R:
(2006*) Hell In The Holy Land,*
The University Press of Kentucky,
U.S.A.

Volunteer Witness Statements 1919-1922 to the Bureau of Military History

Witness Statement No: 1,296:   Tom ' Con' Costello

Witness Statement No: 1,337:   David Daly

Witness Statement No: 1,361:   Gerald Davis

Witness Statement No: 1,594:   Thomas Kieran

Witness Statement No: 1,336:   Patrick Lennon

Witness Statement No: 1,500:   Anthony McCormack

Witness Statement No: 1,503:   Michael McCormack

Witness Statement No: 1,308:   Henry O'Brien

Witness Statement No: 1,309:   Frank O'Connor

Witness Statement No: 1,296:   Seamus O'Meara

Witness Statement No: 1,593:   James Reilly

O generations of freedom remember us, the generations of the vision

(Liam Oisin Kelly)

Phil Tomkins was born in Dublin, Ireland and educated at CBS Westland Row. Dublin. In 2008 he was awarded a BA Hons Degree in Creative Writing by the University of Bolton, England, UK. An ex-elite forces soldier, his writing reflects continuing interest in military history. He currently resides in the North of England, in semi-retirement with his wife Maree.

Photograph courtesy Irish Army, Custume Barracks. Athlone

Footnote: The armour car in the above photograph was on escort duty with General Michael Collins when he was killed during an ambush by Anti-Treaty forces at Beal-na-mBlath, County Cork on the 21 August 1922.